# My Soulful Home

A Year in Flowers

Learn to grow, care for, design and arrange 12 months of flowers.

Published by Passageway Press, an imprint of FB &c Ltd. London.
Company number 08720141.

www.PassagewayPress.com

Cover design by Michelle Freer, cover photography by Trish Reda

ISBN 978-1-334-99908-6

*First Edition*

*To my parents who are the earth to my flower.*

*To my husband who is the water.*

*To my daughters who are the sunshine.*

*I love and thank you all, and Emmett too, for bringing so much joy to our "garden"!*

# CONTENTS

# INTRODUCTION

I want you to live with the beauty of flowers surrounding you. There is no doubt that flowers elevate the everyday. Whether you grow flowers, buy them at the market, or pick them on the side of the road, this book will teach you how to care for, design, and arrange your blooms to best effect.

There are some very straightforward principles and rules to keep in mind while working with flowers. These we will cover in depth so you are comfortable applying them to your designs.

Armed with the understanding of the principles and rules that I share, you will have the confidence to create beautiful arrangements for yourself, family, friends, and events.

Together we dive into twelve tutorials, one for each month of the year. These are meant to provide inspiration and act as a springboard to your own ideas and creations.

I am so glad you have joined me in elevating the everyday with flowers. It is a good way to live. Let's begin right now...

# CHAPTER ONE: THE POWER OF FLOWERS

Each flower is a miracle: pushing out from a seed, transforming from a straggly bare root, then exploding with intricacy, color and scent. The transformation of a flower from its humble beginnings to exquisite beauty and strength is nothing short of miraculous.

Even the smallest blossom in a jelly jar has the power to change a room, the air and one's outlook. Put a sprig of honeysuckle, a gardenia, lilac, orange blossom, or any other flower by your bedside if you aren't sure I am right.

These mini miracles are ours to hold and behold, so why not make flowers a staple in your home? It is easy to do. I promise that surrounding yourself with flowers will make everyday life sweeter. Don't think of floral arrangement as only for special occasions—think of life as one big special occasion and add flowers daily!

In the following chapters, I will teach you the principles of floral design, share information on a variety of flowers, and provide tutorials for twelve arrangements. The goal in writing this book is to impart the skills and confidence to you to create beautiful arrangements that you can enjoy all year long, gift to friends and maybe even plant the seed for a new career.

Before we delve into the specifics, I share with you this thought:

**"Don't spend your life waiting for someone to send you flowers.
Make your own arrangements."**

# CHAPTER TWO: A LITTLE HISTORY

Designing flowers connects you to ancient civilizations. The Egyptians, Greeks and ancient Chinese were not doing most of what we do today, but they were designing and using florals to elevate their everyday and especially for special occasions. They just weren't snapping pictures of what they designed with their phones before the event started!

The use of florals as decoration was first documented with the Egyptians of 2800 B.C. That crowd even used flowers on banquet tables to enhance the dining experience!

The Greeks (600—150 B.C.) came up with a clever container: the horn of plenty. The horn of plenty, or cornucopia, was filled with flowers and fruits and used as table decor. This symbol of abundance remains relevant today.

Flowers in vases began with the Chinese around 207 B.C. The Renaissance and Baroque periods in Europe ushered in floral design as we know it today, made evident in the paintings of those eras, depicting lush flowers arranged in vessels, baskets and the like.

It is believed that the first retail shop dedicated solely to the design of flowers was opened in London in 1876. A Miss Moyses opened Moyses Stevens at 146 Victoria Street Belgravia. Florists to the Crown and countless other people of taste and good fortune, Moyses Stevens is still in business today with several locations in London.

In post-World War I America, floral design gained popularity. Membership in garden clubs began as people had more leisure time and sought a bit of everyday luxury in the form of flowers. After World War II, more efficient transport from overseas introduced exotic blooms to the American floral enthusiasts.

My personal history with flowers dates not quite so far back in the world's timeline. I was about ten years old when my fascination with flowers began. My mother is a gardener, so beautiful blooms surrounded our house. While I don't remember cutting them often for indoor bouquets, I do remember the garden and going to the local nursery with my mom.

I loved going to the nursery with my mother. She would tell me what she was looking to add to her garden and every once in a while we would be in the market to get my grandma her favorite plant. It was this plant that sealed the deal for me. After seeing it, I had to have flowers in my life always.

In the garden nursery there were flowers and greens in every hue for as far as my eye could see. My mother would head off looking for what was on her mental list. It was one of the very few places she didn't insist I stay right by her side. Maybe she was lost in the beauty of it all too. I guess it seemed a pretty safe place for a little girl to go exploring.

Walking into the covered greenhouse, I was met with that humid air and the exotic (to me at the time), flowers, such as orchids. Wandering around picking up dropped flowers and petals from the ground, I would fashion a little bouquet. The first time I did this, I remember my mom saying, upon seeing my creation, "You didn't pick those, did you?" The owner was nearby and he called over, "No, she is helping me tidy up the place." From then on, my bouquets were a mandatory part of a visit.

My grandma's favorite flower was fuchsia. My mom would take care to pick out the very best hanging fuchsia basket. Enough open flowers so it looked beautiful, but enough buds so my grandma would enjoy it long after she took it home with her. Are you familiar was fuchsia flowers? Well they are the flowers of a little girl's dream. Vibrantly pink and shaped like scalloped bells, zillions of them dangling from a deep green plant. I recall thinking, "how could anything be so beautiful?"

Those trips to the garden nursery with my mom and the sight of those fuchsia flowers convinced me that if there was such beauty in the world, I wanted to surround myself with it. And not just sometimes or just for special occasions. Why keep the best up on a shelf for only certain times? Take it down, enjoy it: breathe it in, make it part of your everyday. That is what I decided to do with flowers and I what I hope you do too.

In our current fast paced, technology-driven culture, floral design is a welcome respite. Taking the time to soak in the beauty, the balance, the scent, the 'mini miracles' brought together to create the arrangement is not only welcomed—it is needed.

Breathing in the scent of a tuberose, marveling at the lusciousness of a peony, gazing upon the dazzling color is time well spent. For me, growing, working with, and learning about flowers recharges my battery. I get lost in the beauty. I venture to say, you feel the same way as you are reading this book. So let's join together and with those who came before us and delve further into the beauty that floral design brings to our lives and those of others. Let the fast paced world fall away for a bit while we create beauty. That being said, snapping pictures of your creations with your phones is encouraged. I want to see what you make!

# CHAPTER THREE: PRINCIPLES AND RULES

Principles and rules have a place in all aspects of society, business, and the universe at large. Floral design is no exception. Although it is an art taking form from nature, at the hand of creative souls, floral design is also guided by principles and rules. That doesn't mean a principle doesn't get bent or a rule broken now and again. But before bending or breaking, you need a solid understanding. That is exactly what you will get in this chapter.

Let's examine the general principles of good design and my six essential rules for gorgeous floral arranging. First, learn how to apply these principles and rules to your work, then think about how to be a rebel with a corsage.

The general principles of design play a role in creating beautiful floral arrangements. These principles are:

PROPORTION

HARMONY

COLOR

TEXTURE

SUITABILITY

BALANCE

RHYTHM

Applying these principles to floral design, I have developed my six essential rules for gorgeous floral design. My six essential rules weren't decided upon in a vacuum, nor did they come to me out of the blue. Through reading, observing (and moreover, practicing), I developed techniques that have proven to work every time with any flowers and with any container.

When you learn, understand and practice my six essential and simple rules, you will be able to create beautiful floral designs time and time again. It isn't magic. Well, the flowers are magical, so I guess we floral designers are magicians of sorts. But like any magician there are rules to follow, techniques to understand and practice makes perfect. We will use these six rules throughout the book as a reference and guide.

# SIX ESSENTIAL RULES FOR FLORAL DESIGN:

PICK ONE "WOW" FLOWER

VARY THE TEXTURE

VARY THE SIZE OF THE FLOWERS

CREATE DEPTH

ACHIEVE RHYTHM/FLOW

CHOOSE A COMPLIMENTARY CONTAINER

Let's have a deeper look at each of my six rules. Learning each, understanding the "why", and practicing will allow you to create stunning arrangements. I promise.

There is nothing left to chance if you take a bit of time to grasp the purpose behind the rules. Then, through practice, learn to implement them. This understanding and practice may even result in a decision to break some of the rules now and again to achieve a certain look. But before you get to that point in your floral designing, let's really learn my six essential rules. In the next chapter we examine each rule.

# CHAPTER FOUR: SIX ESSENTIAL RULES OF FLORAL DESIGN

For me, simple is better and, honestly, I don't like lots of rules. So saying I have "rules" for you kind of goes against my grain. But these rules will make floral design simpler, even more enjoyable, and give you predictably stunning results every time.

Not predictable in an FTD sort of way. Rather, predictable in that after mastering my essential rules you can rely on the fact that every bunch of flowers you get your hands on will turn into a heart stopping work of art. You ready for that? I knew you would be...so let's learn the rules.

## RULE 1: PICK A "WOW" FLOWER

Every show needs a star—a central figure that shines brightest and makes the others the better for it. Your floral designs are no exception. Each arrangement needs a special flower that commands attention. Limit the quantity to a few and use an odd numbers (three or five). Limiting the quantity of these "wow" flowers is a good idea for economy's sake too, as they are usually more expensive than the supporting players.

## RULE 2: VARY THE TEXTURE

This gives interest to the arrangement. Pair ruffled petals with spiky ones, lacy capped flowers with sturdy ones. The juxtaposition of varied textures gives life to the design.

## RULE 3: VARY THE SIZE OF THE FLOWERS

Varying the size of the blooms creates interest similar to varied textures. Small and medium sized flowers accent the "wow" flowers. They complement and do not compete like a container full of wow flowers would. Too many divas in the vase is never a good thing!

## RULE 4: CREATE DEPTH

Depth is created by pushing some stems further into the container and letting others stand away a bit. Construct your arrangements so the flowers are not all on the same level. Depth can also be achieved by placing the smallest flowers around the edge of the arrangement. Positioning the smaller flowers there encourages the eye to travel from the "wow" flowers, to the medium sized blooms, to the smallest at the edges. Not to say that all the small flowers should be at the edge when you are creating depth in this manner—small flowers should be scattered throughout the arrangement as well as concentrated at the edges.

## RULE 5: ACHIEVE FLOW

Flow in an arrangement is very pleasing to the human eye. When color and texture are repeated or carried throughout, the eye passes from one spot to the next, taking in the whole of the design. This creates cohesiveness within the design.

Achieving flow is easier than it may seem. Choose a limited palette as well as a limited number of types of flowers. Then repeat each throughout the arrangement in balance. Using an odd number of colors and flowers helps achieve flow, as does a fairly even distribution of each throughout the design.

## RULE 6: CHOOSE A COMPLIMENTARY CONTAINER

The flowers are the stars, not the container. A general rule of thumb is that the container should be one-third the height of the flowers or less. Oftentimes, a nondescript container is best when creating a large number of arrangements for an event. For the one-off arrangement, or those in which you want to carry the theme throughout the florals and container, make sure the vessel enhances the overall look.

Empowered by the understanding of my six essential rules of floral design, you can create stunning arrangements over and over again. You now know the formula! Floral design is an art. As with any art, deviating from the rules sometimes produces the most amazing work. Though I am not a fan of rules for the sake of rules, I am a firm believer in mastering rules that work before breaking any.

My six essential rules of floral design work: they are the framework for success that you can apply again and again. As such, the floral tutorials we will work on together here will apply my six rules. Before we get to the tutorials, let's fully discuss caring for the flowers so the designs you create last as long as possible.

# CHAPTER FIVE: CARING FOR CUT FLOWERS

My six essential rules revolve around the art of floral design. However, there is a scientific component too. The science has to do with the flowers themselves, their ability to stay fresh, and how you, as a floral designer, should handle the flowers in order to prolong the lifespan of your arrangements. Not the most fun part of floral design, but again, very important to understand. The last thing you want is to create a gorgeous arrangement only to wake up to wilted flowers —so let's delve into how to care for cut flowers.

I think the fact that it isn't permanent —almost fleeting, really —is what makes floral design such a special art. It is truly in the moment. Enjoy it now, as it won't last. But that doesn't mean we can't take certain steps to make the moment last a bit longer.

I have several tips to share with you to help you properly care for (and prolong the lifespan of) your arrangements. Tips you should learn and then can decide which and when to employ. Sometimes hurrying in from the market and plopping a bouquet straight into a vase is all we can do. But when you have the time and when it matters that your arrangements last a while, recall my tips or refer to this book.

Just like I stressed with my six essential rules of floral design, learn the best practices for caring for fresh cut flowers, then decide what feels right for you in the moment. After all, flowers are for your enjoyment, not to create more burdensome work. I will explain to you what works best to keep florals fresh and you can decide what to incorporate into your floral design routine.

16

The science of post-harvest flowers is quite simple. Above all, they need to stay hydrated. The ability for the flowers to take up water is the single most important factor in prolonging the life of the arrangement. The water is transported upward through the xylem (plant tissue). This is true for rooted plants and cut flowers. The xylem must not be closed off or damaged so as to prevent the upward flow of water. If this happens, your flowers will have a shortened life span.

To keep the xylem open and carrying water it is a good idea to trim your flower stems with a sharp knife or specially designed floral shears. Using a knife or floral shears instead of scissors or a handheld pruner prevents squishing and closing the xylem.

A note on your tools and container: both must be very clean. Dirty tools or containers breed bacteria. Bacteria will enter the stems of your flowers and cause blockage. Blockage prevents water from flowing upward. Without water, the life of your arrangement is cut short. This is a common sense tip, but worth mentioning.

The best trimming practice is to cut the stems one inch above the bottom. Make the cut on a 45-degree angle under water using a sharp knife or floral shears. The cut should be at an angle so as to give the open end of the stem more exposure to the water.

Angled cuts provide an increased surface area and inhibit the natural sealing of the stem, so more water can be transported up to the flower head. More water to the head of the flower results in fresher arrangements. In addition, cutting on angle creates a point so the stems sit on point on the bottom of the container (not flat). If they are cut flat, the stem could land flush on the bottom of the vase, making water absorption much more challenging. So, make a point to be on point with most flowers. We will discuss the exceptions further on in the book.

To cut your stems, place the flowers in a basin of lukewarm water in the sink. Make the angled cut while the stems are under water if you feel comfortable doing so. If not, make a quick cut out of water and put the stems immediately in a container filled with clean, treated (we'll talk more about that in a minute) lukewarm water.

Whether you are cutting in or out of water, pay attention to where the nodes are on the stems. Nodes are the bumps on the stems where the leaves would emerge. Make your cut directly above a node. Cutting right below or across a node impedes water absorption. Since it is all about getting water to the flowers quickly, making note of the nodes is a good idea.

Did you notice I said "lukewarm water"? Even though common sense might suggest that cold water is best to freshen flowers, this is scientifically not the case for about 95% of the flowers you will be arranging. When a flower prefers cool water, I will make note of it for you.

So why lukewarm water? Warm water molecules move faster than cold ones. Therefore, the warm water molecules scurry up the stem faster getting to the head of the flowers more quickly, providing the needed hydration. Exception to using warm water is when you are working with chrysanthemums, orchids or bulb flowers, like tulips. These flowers prefer cold water.

Cutting the flowers under water and immediately placing into a container of water prevents air bubbles from getting into the stem and prevents the stem from sealing up. If air gets in, water absorption is decreased. If the stem seals up, no water can get up to the stem at all.

While cutting with a sharp knife or floral shears at an angle and underwater may sound like a surgical procedure, it really is not much different than what you do now. If you are cutting with household scissors, switch to a sharp knife or floral shears. If you aren't cutting under water, simply fill up a basin or plug the sink and trim away.

If cutting under water feels awkward to you, make a swift cut out of water and get the stems into water immediately. A swift cut and immediate plonk into water will also go a long way to preserving your flowers.

Clearly, water is key to a floral arrangement's life span. But not just any water. Should you get your water tested or buy distilled water for your arrangements? The answer: probably not, unless you are creating centerpieces for an event, starting a floral design business, or you *really* really want your bouquets to last a long time.

Since knowledge is power, I will share information with you on the best type of water for your arrangements. What you choose to do with that information is up to you. For the most part, clean tap water is sufficient, but not perfect for florals. For example: if your clean tap water is softened, the sodium in the water may be toxic to some flowers (such as roses and carnations). Fluoride in water is toxic to gerber daisies, gladiolus, and freesia. In addition, high concentrations of dissolved minerals in the water may clog up the flow of water up the stem of any flower.

Most tap water is sufficient, but not perfect for the reasons mentioned above, and moreover, because it is too neutral. Flowers prefer water with a bit of acid in it. The ideal pH level is 3.0 - 4.5. Acidic water is taken up the xylem more readily than neutral water.

The level of acidity in the water is easily increased by adding a floral preservative (this is what I was referring to a few paragraphs ago about treated water). When I refer to "treated water" as we go on, I am referring to water mixed with a floral preservative. Simply follow the directions on the jar of preservative to get the proper amounts. In a following chapter, I cover floral preservatives in detail.

After making the cuts, place the flowers in water. You need to let the flowers rehydrate. This is of greater importance for commercially purchased flowers, rather than those cut from your own garden.

Commercially purchased flowers may have travelled long distances without proper hydration before getting to your local shop. Then, if you are like me, you do ten more errands after picking up a few bouquets while grocery shopping. These flowers sorely need a fresh cut, hydration, and time to soak up the water before you start fussing with them to arrange. Or you may have purchased flowers online. These beauties certainly need some TLC upon arrival.

To rehydrate your flowers before arranging, simply place them in treated water and put them in a cool, dark place for two to six hours (longer is better—if you can wait more than two hours, do so). Strong-stemmed flowers, like roses, like to condition in deep water. Soft, fleshy-stemmed blooms (such as bulb flowers) prefer shallow water.

If you must get to your arranging right away, so be it, but like the other advice I am sharing, waiting until the flowers have fully re-hydrated is the best practice. Ahh, but in life, best practices are not always possible. Just do the best you can to hold off as long as you can to let the flowers revive themselves. I know you have tons of other stuff to do anyway!

If the flowers were purchased at the grocery store and you want to arrange them as quickly as possible, at the very least cut them properly as soon as you get in the door, place them in water with a preservative mixed in, and let them sit for the time it takes you to put away the groceries. At a minimum, this will give time for them to soak up a bit of fresh water and nutrients before the arranging begins. Do the flowers and you this small favor.

I have referred to floral preservative and treating your water with such preservatives. I will discuss that in depth shortly, but before we get to that subject, let's take a look at a few flowers that will need a bit of special attention right away to survive in an arrangement. It is nothing too taxing on you, the arranger, but must be taken into account when working with certain flowers.

# CHAPTER SIX: SOME FLOWERS NEED SPECIAL ATTENTION

The flowers that need special attention are not particularly exotic. They are actually rather common, so you may find yourself often working with them to create arrangements. That being the case, I want to share with you a few tips on working with these beauties. The types of flowers that need special attention to which I refer are those that have hollow stems, and those that give off a sap when cut. These flowers need to be handled differently than flowers with solid stems and those that do not emit a sap when cut.

Flowers with hollow stems need a little help getting and keeping the water flowing upward, as air gets in and gravity brings the water down. You can help by cutting these hollow-stemmed flowers straight across (NOT on a 45 degree angle like solid-stemmed flowers). In the case of large enough hollow-stemmed flowers, you should turn the flower upside down and slowly fill the stem with water. This will expel any air (which would prevent the water from getting to the flower) and immediately provide water to the flower head. After filling the stem, hold the bottom with your finger and slide into a vase of treated water.

It is even suggested to plug the stems of wide hollow-stemmed flowers with a tiny bit of cotton to prevent air from re-entering the stem, slow the release of the water down the stem, and still allow fresh water to be absorbed. Frankly, this is bit too much special attention for me, but hey, if your sister's wedding centerpieces are made of hollow-stemmed delphiniums and you are her florist, break out the cotton balls!

Hollow-stemmed flowers can draw up the water—think of their stems as a drinking straw.

So, it is not so much fighting gravity that is the issue. It is the fact that air bubbles often get lodged in these hollow stems. These air bubbles block the water so the stems require the special attention I outlined. If the upward flow of water is blocked, the flowers droop and wilt. Despite all efforts, sometimes air is trapped in a flower stem. Aha, but there is a trick to releasing the air trapped in a hollow stem. I learned this trick from a special lady many years ago. Want me to share it? *My pleasure...*

Having just finished college and while awaiting admission to law school, I secured myself a work visa and headed off to London. As luck would have it, I found a job as a legal assistant and an amazing flat in Notting Hill. How I landed that job at a firm in Mayfair I will never really know. My typing was terrible and I had no legal education yet. I was really good at answering the phone, receiving packages, making tea and, you guessed it—arranging the flowers for the reception area.

The firm had a client who whisked in about every two weeks with her little dog under her arm. Her perfume would waft into the reception area (where I sat) moments before she arrived. Hers was an enchanting musky rose-scented calling card. She was of a certain age, as they say. In appearance, she was a cross between Carolyne Roehm and Gloria Vanderbilt...and maybe a dash of Wallis, Duchess of Windsor.

Her manner was worldly and sophisticated. But the best thing about her was that she made you feel like you were the reason she was put on planet earth. She was so utterly charming, gracious, and genuinely interested in everyone—even me, a young American girl, clacking away key by key on the keyboard. To me, she was absolutely marvelous.

One rainy day when she was leaving the office, I was trying in vain to revive a vase of tulips that had drooped dramatically. Having just bought them the day before with the weekly office flower budget, I was determined to fluff them back to health. She saw what I was doing as she readied herself to go out into the rain. Before slipping on her A-line trench, she placed her pooch on my chair, removed the gold pin from her lapel and began piercing each tulip where the stem met the flower. Just then the phone rang, I was jolted into answering it. Working swiftly, she repositioned her pin, slipped on her trench and picked up her dog as I looked at her in wonder. "A bit of magic, just watch," she said, and was off with a "bye, love". In what seemed like seconds after the heavy wooden door shut tight behind her, the tulips began to rise and stand tall again.

I never saw her again (as my visa expired ten days later and it was time to head home), but her magic trick stayed with me. Like many things in life, I came to understand that her trick wasn't magic after all. Her golden pinprick simply released the air in the hollow stem of the tulips so the water could get to the flowers. Not magic, but she was magical nonetheless.

# Common Hollow-stemmed Flowers

Amaryllis

Daffodils

Agapanthus

Lupines

Delphiniums

Tulips

Alliums

Gerbera

Larkspur

Hollyhocks

I have no marvelous women or magic tricks to share when talking about flowers that emit a sap. I could say it is sticky subject, but I wouldn't do that. The fact is that sappy, oozy stems are quite easily dealt with boiling water or a flame: you just need to seal up the stem. "Cauterize" is probably the correct term to use, but as I think cauterize is foul word, let's use "seal". Seal up the sappy stem by holding it under boiling water or over a flame for a few seconds. Done! In doing so, you are not preventing water from getting up the stem. You are preventing the sap from hardening and closing off the opening of the stem. Water can still rise if you seal the end.

Sappy flowers lose significant moisture when they are cut from the plant. In some cases, the plant sap begins to ooze from the cut stem immediately. This ooze will continue until it fully blocks the end of the stem. In the meantime, substantial moisture is lost. This, of course, puts the flower at risk of wilting in your arrangement. Plant sap can also be toxic to other flowers in the arrangement.

Let me take a moment here to mention that sweet yellow daffodils contain sap that is toxic to other flowers. That sap prevents other flowers from taking up water. This is a bit of a problem as daffodils have...what? That's right, *hollow stems*. Therefore, you can't seal them up. The toxic sap slides out and into the container water, poisoning the other flowers. So you should keep your daffodils separate, but equal. They look pretty in a single flower arrangement anyway.

If you must mix daffodils into an arrangement, try this method: let the daffodils sit alone in water alone for three hours, then change the water and give it another three hours. Thereafter, it may be safe to mix them with other flowers. Do not re-cut their stems before doing so or you will need to start the process over *six more hours*! If the arrangement is for a special occasion why take the risk? I have a tutorial to share that I think you will love using just daffodils. Think of them as loners.

# COMMON SAPPY STEMMED FLOWERS

POPPIES

DAFFODILS

SUNFLOWER

HOLLYHOCKS

ZINNIA

HYACINTH

DAHLIAS

TULIPS (SAPPY AND HOLLOW)

HYDRANGEA (SAPPY AND WOODY)

# Chapter Seven: Floral Preservatives

To be as long lasting as possible cut flowers need three things besides water. These three things are: carbohydrates, biocides and acidifiers. Carbohydrates are necessary for cell metabolism. Biocides ward off bacteria and promote general health and the acidifiers alter the pH of the water to increase water absorption.

You can provide for these three needs by adding a commercially produced floral preservative or adding your own preservative recipe/home remedy to the water. Adding a floral preservative to the water before placing the freshly cut stems in the vase or container will markedly increase the life span of the flowers. Simply follow the directions on the jar so you use the correct amount.

Floral preservative in small packets often come with market bouquets. Before adding floral preservation to the water, check the label for proper amounts. More is not better, and less than necessary will be ineffective. Add the commercial preservative to the container before you fill with water and mix well.

I don't always have floral preservative on hand, but I do have a pantry stocked with the right ingredients to replicate the effects of using one. A recipe that I use, which mimics the positive effects of a purchased floral preservative is the following:

- one quart lukewarm water

- one teaspoon white sugar

- one teaspoon chlorine bleach

- two teaspoons lemon or lime juice

As with the commercial floral preservatives, mix the ingredients in this recipe with the water well before adding in the flowers.

Another home mixture that conditions the water like a floral preservative is to add a twelve-ounce can of clear lemon/lime soda and one tablespoon of chlorine bleach to a gallon of water. Don't use sugar-free soda—your flowers crave the sugar/carbs. The citrus soda provides the acid and sugar while the chlorine bleach inhibits the bacteria.

Vodka and a teaspoon of sugar is touted as a floral preservative too. Adding vodka to the water will aid in keep the flowers fresh, but does not inhibit bacteria. Oddly, vodka works in the opposite way on flowers as it does on people. If you see your flowers drooping, add vodka and they will stand tall again. Adding vodka to people usually doesn't have that effect!

In a pinch, dropping a U.S. penny in the water will lower the pH level. This is due to the copper in pennies. Look for pennies made before 1982, as those have higher concentrations of copper. Adding a penny provides one-third of the equation—it increases the acidity of the water.

Aspirin is also claimed to be a floral preservative. The salicylic acid in aspirin will help keep the water clean and free from bacteria. Vodka, pennies, and aspirin do not give cut flowers all they need to last a good long time. That being said, they each help a bit and can't hurt.

If you are serious about having your flowers last as long as possible, you should make sure to add a commercial floral preservative or mix up the home recipe I shared. Make this part of your routine each and every time you are arranging flowers. It is very simple to do and will most definitely increase the life span of your arrangements.

Keep a container of floral preservative under the sink and/or the ingredients on hand. If you make it easy to treat the water, you most likely will do it. I also keep a little bag of the extra packets of floral preservative that come with many market bouquets. When buying a few bunches of flowers, I will not use each and every packet. I may only need one depending on the size of the vase I am using. I simply tuck the leftover packets into a little bag and keep those under my sink for next time. Then I just cut open the little packet and pour. Easy!

Now, if treating the water as I suggest seems like too much effort for you, simply change the water every third day. Changing the water is the easiest and most overlooked way to extend the life of flowers. You should do this even if you use a preservative, but most certainly if you do not. No matter your water's pH level or the amount of sugar in the mix, if the water is dirty, the stems cannot conduct it efficiently. So whether you decide not to use preservative, buy cases of lemon/lime soda, sneak shots of vodka for your flowers, or keep a roll of U.S. pennies on hand, just change the water at least every three days. That simple step alone will go a long way to preserving your flowers.

Proper cutting, the right water, giving the cut flowers time to rest and absorb water, changing the water frequently, and using a floral preservative are steps every floral designer should be knowledgeable of and take when practical. I have included a simple checklist for cut flower longevity. You'll find it on the following page and again at the very end of the book. You can use it as quick reference reminder until the steps to long lasting flowers are so ingrained that you no longer need to check. I know that will be really soon, but if you ever need me and my checklist I've got you covered.

In the next chapter, we'll talk all about harvesting flowers from your garden. I will guide you through the step-by-step instruction on how to best to harvest from outside your own door. Details on post-harvest garden flower care are covered. I also provide you with a list of the best flowers to plant for a cutting garden. Lucky are those who have even the tiniest of gardens to tend! We'll head out to the garden in a minute, but before we do take a look at the checklist.

# CHECKLIST FOR LONG LASTING CUT FLOWERS

- ☐ Buy the freshest flowers you can get your hands on.

- ☐ Prepare a container of treated lukewarm water. Use cool water for orchids, chrysanthemums, bouvardia, and bulb flowers.

- ☐ Let flowers sit in a cool, dark place to rehydrate for a minimum of two hours.

- ☐ Fill the display vase/container with treated water.

- ☐ If necessary, make second cut for the arrangement in the same manner as first cut. Do not recut daffodils.

- ☐ Design: have fun!

- ☐ Stand back and admire!

- ☐ Change the water and add fresh preservative every three days.

# CHAPTER EIGHT: HARVESTING GARDEN FLOWERS

It is a bit painful: you plant, nurture, tend and fuss, then you cut! Some might say, "No way!" But cutting your precious flowers saves them from nature's wrath, so you can enjoy the fruits of your labor indoors for a spell. Better still, cutting also promotes more flowering. So cut away!

Even if you find it difficult to cut the flowers in your garden, you must admit it is quite satisfying to feast your eyes on a homegrown vase of flowers on your counter. If you are squeamish about cutting your beauties, realize you don't have to cut too many. Just a few mixed with some greenery is enough to make a beautiful arrangement. And in reward for your bravery in cutting, the plants will be working on new flowers while you are inside admiring your arrangement.

If you are venturing out to the garden to cut, make sure you are doing it at the right time and in the right way. You want these sacrificed beauties to last a long time. The best time to harvest flowers from your garden is in the early morning. This is the time the flowers are freshest. They have had the benefit of the cool evening/night temperatures and received a dose of morning dew.

Throughout the day, plants lose moisture through their leaves. Their stems are weakened and flowers may appear droopy. Cutting in that state will not give your bouquet the best start and will most likely ensure that it is short lived. So head out to the garden in the early morning. That sounds delightful anyway, doesn't it?

Bring along a sharp knife or floral shears for the initial cut. As discussed, do not use household scissors to cut your flowers. This type of scissor is set to cut paper and such, not the bulk of a stem. Hence household scissors will more than likely crush (or at the very least damage) the vascular system, inhibiting water from getting up the stem.

Without the proper intake of water, your cut flower is doomed to a short life. You won't cut paper with your fabric scissor (and I bet you would chase down anyone who tried)! So, don't cut your flowers with household scissors. Get yourself a tool designed for this purpose and keep it with your garden gloves for easy access.

Okay, so you are just about to head out the door to cut a beautiful bouquet. It's early—arm yourself with a coffee or tea for you and a plastic bucket filled with several inches of lukewarm water for your cuttings. Bring a bucket of cool water if you are harvesting bulb flowers, orchids, chrysanthemums or bouvardia. Use plastic buckets if possible; metal ones might mess with the pH of the water.

Cut a stem and place it into the bucket right away. Sip your tea or coffee after a stem hits the water, not in between cut and bucket. Even a few moments out of the water after a cut can inhibit the flower's ability to soak up water. A cut stem out of water will immediately begin to close up.

If you are cutting daffodils or any other flowers in the narcissus family (such as jonquils), bring out a separate container for them. These flowers omit a sap that is toxic to other flowers. You might say they are narcissists because it is all about them.

Enjoy the morning, but make it snappy in getting the cut stems into the water. Once in the water, have a look around, breathe in the scent, watch a hummingbird having breakfast and listen to the hum of the bees. You have created a slice of heaven - enjoy it! Then when you are ready, bring some of it inside.

When cutting flowers from your garden for arrangements it is useful to take into consideration the stages of a flower's bloom, so you know when it is best to make the cut for full floral effect in your arrangement. No one wants a vase full of unopened buds. So, keep the following in mind when choosing which flowers to cut and when.

Flowers with many buds on a stem or branch need to have at least one bud almost open and at least one unfurled enough to show some color before it is advisable to make a cut. If the buds are still too tightly closed when the stem is cut, they simply will not open. This is good to know as well for those arrangements that you may want to accent with some sweet closed buds. But a whole vase full of unopened buds is a disappointment.

Individual stemmed flowers need to be fully open before cutting. These flowers will not continue the blooming process once detached from the mother plant. This being said, some arrangements are enhanced by the addition of buds. So if this is a look you want to go for in your arrangement, by all means cut when budded. Just know the buds will remain and not open in water.

All this talk of buds makes me think of forcing branches. This is a stunning and sometimes dramatic way of using buds in floral arrangements. Let's go over how you can force budding branches to bloom in the next chapter.

# CHAPTER NINE: FORCING BRANCHES TO BLOOM

Growing up, our Cape Cod style house had a side garden filled with forsythia bushes. I loved how their bright sunny yellow blossoms brightened up even the dreariest New York late winter day and, moreover, that they signaled the coming of spring. Whenever I see forsythia branches in the market I bring home a few bundles. They remind me of being a little girl, and as they do not grow here in Southern California, they are a treat for me.

Forsythia and many other flowering deciduous shrubs and trees need a period of cold weather to go dormant, and then they re-bloom. The buds are often formed the season before and endure the cold with the branches. It doesn't get cold enough where I live for several of the flowering shrubs and trees I listed below to bloom (such as my childhood forsythia) but some, like redbuds, do grow naturally here.

If it is cold where you live, force branches from your property by heading out midday (not early morning as with cutting flowers). Pick a sunny afternoon in midwinter to hunt for the perfect branches. By midwinter, the buds will be formed and gone through requisite cold period in order to bloom. By cutting branches for forcing in midday, the buds will not be frozen and brittle. Really cold buds won't adjust as readily to the warm temperatures inside. If you live where it is warm and have trees with buds to force (such as redbuds), any time of day is fine for harvesting.

Look for branches about a half-inch in diameter with several buds. Buds that are round and fat are flower buds. Buds that are small and pointed are leaf buds. If the branches are over one-half inch in diameter, you will have to split them a bit. I will explain that in a moment.

Cut the branches on a 45-degree angle with a sharp clean tool and place in a bucket of lukewarm water, just like you would with cut flowers. Once you have collected enough to make a statement arrangement, take your bounty inside. Leaving the branches submerged in the water, make a fresh angled cut on the smaller branches.

For those branches with wider diameters, split up the bottom one to four inches using a pruner, shears, or a sharp knife. Then, make a fresh 45-degree cut one inch from the bottom of the wider branches that you just split. If this seems too much to do under water, work quickly on a cutting board or other surface, cutting, splitting and replacing the freshly cut branches in lukewarm water. Cuts made indoors should be made with the vase/container height in mind. The indoor cut is akin to cutting fabric: measure twice, cut once.

Prepare the vase/container with lukewarm water and thoroughly mix in a floral preservative. Store bought or a home recipe will work just fine. Before settling the branches in the vase, remove the lower foliage and buds that would be below the water line. This prevents rotting and growth of bacteria. Always nice to prevent that sort of thing!

Place the branches in the treated water and arrange as you like. In a short time the buds will start to unfurl and spring will have sprung in your house! It is best to keep this type of arrangement away from bright light or a heat source, such as an air vent or working fireplace. Try to mimic the cold temps of the late winter/early spring as much as you can indoors by selecting a spot near a door to the outside, a drafty window or cool spot.

The following is a list of flowering branches that are known to bloom indoors using my tips:

FORSYTHIA

REDBUD

JAPANESE OR FLOWERING QUINCE

FLOWERING DOGWOOD

VERNAL WITCH HAZEL

HAWTHORN

HONEYSUCKLE

SAUCER MAGNOLIA

STAR MAGNOLIA

APPLE AND CRABAPPLE

FLOWERING ALMOND, CHERRY AND PLUM

EUROPEAN PUSSY WILLOW

SPIREA

VIBURNUM

# CHAPTER TEN: BEST CUTTING GARDEN FLOWERS

Well, you can't cut 'em if you don't have 'em. So, I am including a list of some of my favorite cutting garden flowers. Let's keep it a low-maintenance mix of annuals and perennials of differing heights. Keeping the purpose of the garden in mind, flowers with longer stems are a good choice. So as not to have your garden look like the back room at the nursery with a confetti like mix of colors and blooms types, keep the plants to a mix of about six and limit the palette. Remember, these beauties are going to go into vases together. That being said, if you like the look of all the colors mixed together, then toss the confetti!

Choose plants or seeds for your cutting garden that have a range of bloom times—spring, midsummer and late summer. Of course, the best choices are those that keep up the show from spring to fall. Making smart choices will keep your "flower shop" in business all season.

Making smart choices for your cutting garden also includes choosing flowers that thrive in the same conditions. Most flowers suitable for cutting enjoy lots of sun. However, there are several terrific cutting flowers that prefer shade, such as astilbe, lily-of-the-valley, and lady's mantle. Plant them too, if you have room elsewhere—just not mixed in with the sun lovers.

Since we are going low-maintenance, I am suggesting flowering plants that are relatively drought-tolerant and aren't very picky about the soil. That being said, the soil you plant in should be properly amended to give the seeds or plants a healthy environment. We can dish on the dirt in another book, but here let's focus on the flowers.

A three-foot by six-foot bed can hold about twenty plants comfortably. Be mindful that some plants, like dahlias require a lot of room (two-three feet), so limit those space hogs if your bed is on the smaller side. An area on the side of your house is a great place for a small cutting garden. The loss of flowers after you snip won't be as obvious if you plant your garden on the side rather than the front or back. It is nice to have a cutting garden close to the house so it encourages you to cut often and enjoy the blooms while in wait for the vase.

Remember this is a cutting garden we are talking about, so you need to get in there and cut! If the bed is not very deep, you can probably lean in to gather the blooms. If it is deep, you'll need to separate the plants into rows to allow for some walking room. Your cutting garden can still have a lovely layout with the taller plants in the back, medium in the middle, then shorter in front; simply leave a bit of space to get to the back row.

One more thing before we get to the list: garden zones. If you are a gardener you likely know your zone, but in your cutting garden you don't really need to pay attention. You see, garden zones were developed to give gardeners a way of knowing if a plant would thrive in their region. Zone maps are tools that show where various permanent landscape plants can adapt. Two keys words in that sentence: "tools" and "permanent".

Zone maps are tools that you can choose to use, but not be a slave to, as they only really impact permanent plants. Shrubs, perennials, or trees that you obviously wish to be as permanent as possible should be within your zone. This will give these plants the best chance to survive and grow year after year. Annuals and the plants you will use for cutting do not need to be permanent, so you can experiment out of zone. Another wonderful reason to start a cutting garden or expand the one you have!

I have included the zones for the plants I listed for completeness and if you plan to make any of the perennials a permanent part of your landscape. If not, feel free to plant any that strikes your fancy no matter where you garden. Since many are annuals, or can be treated like annuals, you really do not have to concern yourself too much with the zone. If the plant is an annual, any zone will do. The plant lasts only for a season. If a plant is a perennial and does well in your zone it will re-appear next year or remain and bloom again. If a perennial is not suited for your zone, but you want it for your cutting garden, simply treat it like an annual. It's your cutting garden: go ahead and go zone-less!

Now, on to the list. It is not exhaustive, of course, but gives a nice selection of easy care flowers that will reward you with cut bouquets and keep on pumping out the blooms. Plus, long lists can sometimes be overwhelming, don't you think?

Many of these flowering plants can be easily and swiftly grown from seed. Propagating from seed really cuts down on the cost of planting a cutting garden. Low cost as well as low maintenance.

Because I am a gardener, I can' help but add a few words at this point about your soil. Let me be brutally honest, while I think YOU are absolutely fabulous in every way, I know your soil isn't. Nobody's is—not mine, not Martha's, not anybody's. You can accept that truth and do nothing, or do something super easy to change the playing field, so to speak.

Because I know you are a do-er and want to give your flowers the best start possible, I am going to share with you how to easily amend your soil. Then we'll get to the list of what you should plant in your top-notch soil.

Sound good? Now, if you have no intention of growing the flowers for your arrangements skim this section, or skip to Chapter Eleven wherein I talk about why flowers smell (*I love knowing stuff like that, don't you?*).

Okay, so for those getting down in the dirt, let's talk soil amendments. Gardens with unamended soil provide a less than an ideal environment for many plants. Too rocky, scraped bare from new construction, too clay-like, too sandy, the list goes on…

While you can't really change the soil's basic texture, you can improve its structure making it better for your plants. You can do this by simply adding amendments. Kind of like a man (no offense to my male readers): you can't change his innate fashion sense, but you can improve his wardrobe.

PH balance, nitrogen, organic vs. synthetic, granular vs. liquid, when to feed plants, which plants to feed, and all those big bags at the nursery promising award-winning flowers can make gardening seem a lot more complicated than it is quite honestly. You see, it is actually quite simple.

Plants have basic needs just like you and I. While I can't promise you a blue ribbon, you will have a healthy, productive garden with loads of flowers to cut and arrange if you consider and provide for those basic needs. So, what are a plant's basic needs and how can they be easily met? A plant's basic needs are as simple as what follows:

- Healthy, nutritious soil

- Water

- Sun

We'll concern ourselves with the need for high-quality soil here. To provide your plants with a healthy nutritious soil, you must improve the soil you have by working in the best amendment of all: organic matter. It is that simple.

Organic matter is the best amendment for soil of any texture. What is organic matter, you ask? Well, organic matter is kind of "earthy". More specifically, it is decaying remains of plants and animals. Now, I am not suggesting you catch squirrels and bury them in your yard. You can simply buy bags of organic matter and work it into your soil. There are three basic types of organic matter:

- Compost (decomposed food scraps and yard waste)

- Well-rotted manure (need I define further? I'll just say, "Wear gloves".)

- Soil conditioners (combo of several organic amendments sold in bags–think of it as a multivitamin for your soil)

Of course, you can make your own compost or purchase any of the three. Right about now are you asking, "why not just fertilize?" Good question! This is why: fertilizer feeds the plants. Organic matter feeds the soil.

Without healthy nutritious soil, your plants do not have a solid foundation from which to thrive and flower and make you exceedingly happy. So feed the soil—it will eventually feed your soul with beautiful flowers!

Well, let's get on to that list of flowers I promised. The plants on this list produce flowers that are in the mid-sized to small range. I will give you another list with choices of "WOW" flowers further along in the book. All of these plants need about six hours of sun a day to thrive. Most are relatively drought-tolerant as well.

Now remember, do not be hesitant to cut these flowers and bring them indoors to enjoy. That is the whole point! The following are some of my easy care cutting garden favorites.

# Easy Care Cutting Garden Flowers
## For a Sunny Spot

**Globe Amaranth:** Prolific bloomer and easy care are hallmarks of globe amaranth. This annual can be grown from seed. Round pom-pom like blooms in pink, purple and white on green stems. The plant tops out between 6 and 12 inches tall. (Zones 2–11)

**Garden Stock:** This plant grows in tall clusters. Larger and looser than snapdragons, but of a similar look. Garden stock is very reliable in the garden, but prefers cooler temperatures, so enjoy it in the spring. It has a sweet, spicy smell akin to cloves. Cut when the flowers on a spike are two-thirds open for best results in a vase. The blooms are pink, purple, white, and yellow. (Zones 2–11)

**Bachelor Button:** Also known as cornflower. Grows well from seed. This was the first flower I ever grew from seed and wow! Did it grow. Can get wild in fact! These cheery blooms have smallish flowers and enjoy a very long vase life. It is one of the very few true blue flowers and it color is magnificent. Bachelor button also comes in white, red, purple and pink. (Zones 2–11)

**Zinnia:** Doesn't get much easier in the garden than with zinnias. These flowers are annuals that grow well from seed and are drought-tolerant. There are many varieties and colors to choose from, all in vibrant hues. Choose a variety with longer stems for a cutting garden. You will need to scald the stem with boiling water or a flame as zinnias release a sap when cut. (Zones 2–11)

**Salvia:** Carefree, long blooming perennial are the hallmarks of salvia. The plant grows in a clump and produces violet flowers on spiky purple stems. Bees and butterflies delight when you add salvia to your garden. (Zones 4–9)

**Yarrow:** Low-maintenance and drought-tolerant, yarrow is a great addition to a cutting garden. The lacy-capped blooms on sturdy stems are great fillers for arrangements and bouquets. Choices come in yellow, pink, orange and white. (Zones 3–9)

**Colewort:** Another wonderful filler flower is the perennial colewort. It is a strong multi branched plant that produces small white-petalled flowers. It can grow as tall as eight feet and as wide as five feet, so it may be potentially too large for a small cutting bed. If you have the room plant it in the back. (Zones 6 –9)

**Shasta Daisy:** This perennial is a classic cutting garden flower. White multi-petalled blooms on sturdy stems make this plant the perfect choice for your cutting garden bed. Long-lasting in a vase and low maintenance in the garden. (Zones 4–9)

**Cosmos:** Another classic of the cutting bed is the annual cosmos. The stems are not that sturdy, but the blooms are light weight and so cheery. The foliage is wispy and fern like so adds nice texture as well. Easily grown from seed. Cosmos have light and dark pink as well as white blooms. (Zones 2–11)

**Sunflower:** Not the huge headed variety, but a mid-sized sunflower is a perfect addition to an arrangement. There are countless types of sunflowers to choose from (both annual and perennial varieties). All grow well from seed. These flowers last over a week in a vase. Good choices for arrangements are the pollen-less sunflowers, such as Sunbeam, Sunbright, Sunrich Lemon and Orange. The sturdy stems will need to be scalded after cutting, like Zinnias, as the stems release a sap. Hold under boiling hot water or over a flame for a few seconds to seal up the stem. (Zones 4–9)

**Veronica Speedwell:** Sounds more like a heroine than a plant! Veronica speedwell is a flashy spiked perennial flower that is a terrific addition to arrangements. It comes in shades of pink, white and purple. (Zones 3–8)

**Spray Carnation:** Carnations can be annuals, biennials, or perennials. Make life easier and look for a perennial variety if you want to add them to your garden. Carnations have a lowly reputation in floral design, but not for good reason. We'll talk more about that later on in the book. The spray variety with several boom are a stem is particularly lovely. (Zones 5–8)

**Drum Stick Plant:** An unusual but easy-to-grow perennial plant. The bright yellow balls atop strong stems make these flowers resemble xylophone mallets. How fun in an arrangement! (Zones 9–11)

**Blanket Flower:** If you love the colors of autumn, then perennial blanket flower should be in your cutting garden. Very heat and drought-tolerant with long lasting color, blanket flower is an easy care plant. (Zones 3–11)

**Dusty Miller:** This plant is best treated as an annual in my opinion, although in warm zones it can be a perennial. However, it gets very leggy or can grow into a misshapen bush. For cutting garden purposes, treat it as an annual. Dusty miller with its deeply cut foliage and slivery color is a wonderful foil to brightly colored flowers, as well as a compliment to the more pastel hued. Flats of dusty miller are inexpensive and easy to grow. Cutting helps the plants stay compact. (Zones 2–11, or Zones 8–10 as a perennial)

**Lupine:** These tall beauties are short-lived perennials, but since they are for cutting, you may want to add lupines to your garden mix. The flowers come in deep pink, light pink, white, yellow and blue-ish tones. The stalk-like stems can reach from one to four feet. (Zones 4–8)

**Coneflower:** A perennial staple of the cutting garden is the coneflower or echinacea. Strong flower on a sturdy stem, the coneflower will not give you trouble or disappoint in a vase or the garden. (Zones 3–9)

**Garden Phlox:** On tall stems growing to three or four feet high, garden phlox produces trusses of flowers in white, pink, lavender and a sort of blue. It is a perennial. The old time favorite of cutting gardens will thrive in yours. (Zones 3–8)

**Purple Top Verbena:** Resembling statice, purple top verbena produces quarter-inch blooms on stiff coarse stems. This perennial plant can get quite large topping out at six feet tall and 3 feet wide. Blooming all summer into fall, and filling your arrangements over and over again, purple top verbena is a great choice. (Zones 7–11)

**Nasturtium:** Looking for smaller plants? Nasturtium, with its round leaves and two-inch blooms, is a perfect choice. Extremely carefree, attractive to hummingbirds and edible, this perennial plant is a workhorse in the cutting garden. (Zones 4–11)

**Horsemint:** This plant is a multi-branched perennial that serves as a perfect filler flower for your arrangements. It boosts pale pink, lavender, and yellow flowers along its branches and gives off a scent similar to oregano. (Zones 5–10)

**Black-Eyed Susan:** A mainstay of cutting gardens and very cheery in arrangements, black-eyed susan is a terrific addition to your garden. Plant this perennial and you will be rewarded with numerous blooms per branched stem and deep green leaves all summer long. (Zones 3–9)

**Elfin Pink Penstemon:** Thriving in full sun, this small perennial will give your cutting garden a pop of deep pink. A spiky plant with tubular blooms, elfin pink penstemon is a dainty addition to any arrangement. (Zones 4–9)

**Blooming Cilantro:** Heat and drought-tolerant blooming cilantro is a super easy plant to grow, and it adds so much to arrangements. It is "blooming" because you let it flower. Blooming cilantro grows to about three to four feet, so keep it as a backdrop. A favorite of mine is sweet annie, but any variety will do. Fluffy foliage, tiny delicate white flowers and that oh-so-fresh signature scent! You can cook with it, too. For adding to recipes pick a bit before it flowers. Interesting to note, that grown for its leaves this plant is called cilantro. Grown for its spicy seeds, it is called coriander. By either name, it is an annual, but may be mistaken for a perennial in frost-free zones, as it readily self-seeds. I love a plant that does all the work! (Zones 2–11)

**Blue Cap Sea Holly:** Spiny, thistle-like flowers bloom from July through September. Blue cap sea holly is a perennial that adds a whole lot of interest to your garden as well as in arrangements. This flower's texture, color, and its unusual appearance will make a statement. Can be dried as well. (Zones 5–11)

# CHAPTER ELEVEN: WHY AND HOW FLOWERS SMELL?

A beautiful floral arrangement is such a visual delight. Add in a fragrance and you have a tour de force for the senses sitting on your table! I recently had a vase full of tuberoses and other pretty blooms on my dining room table. I couldn't pass by without leaning into the bouquet to breathe in the marvelous scent. I have read that the Victorians forbade young girls from smelling tuberoses for fear they would fall into an "erotic frenzy." Well, let's just say that didn't happen here while that vase was full, but I did enjoy the intoxicating scent a whole lot.

If you have even wondered why and how flowers smell, today is the day that question will be answered. The "why" has nothing to do with people. Even though we benefit from the scents, flowers are not pumping out fragrance for you, me, or those giddy Victorian girls.

While we may delight in the scent of flowers, they aren't doing all the hard work to produce sweet or seductive scents for us. It is for the bugs and the butterflies, the humming birds, the moths, and even the bats.

Flowers produce scent to attract—not people, but rather the pollinators. Bugs, butterflies, hummingbirds, moths, and even bats are creatures that pollinate. All flowers need to be pollinated; it is their end game. So, flowers send off scent to lure the pollinators.

Flowers produce a complex mixture of low-weight compounds that swirl together to create the scents we adore. Some flowers produce this mixture from their petals and some produce from their deeper organs, like orchids do. Emitted into the air, the scents attract pollinators. A "come hither" of the floral variety, if you will.

Like snowflakes, no two floral scents are exactly the same. Each flower, even of the same variety, produces a distinct scent. We might not notice the subtle differences, but the bugs, hummingbirds, butterflies, moths, and bats do.

Scent not only attracts pollinators, but directs them to the right plants for them. For example, flowers pollinated by bees have sweet scents. Those pollinated by beetles have spicy, fruity odors. Pollinators can distinguish between the scents to make their choices, much like we might at a buffet.

Plants maximize their scent when the flowers are ready for pollination. Once sufficiently pollinated, the scent decreases so that other plants in need of pollination can be found. So very civilized and orderly.

Understanding the why and how of floral scents doesn't diminish my delight or fascination. It still seems pretty magical to me. You will want to add scented plants and flowers to your cutting garden, so your arrangements produce not only visual beauty but delight your sense of smell as well. Who knows—the scents may even conjure up a frenzy!

Below is a list of fragrance producing plants that are easy to grow in your sunny cutting garden. Plant a few and then add stems to your arrangements for a double sensory delight!

## Easy Care: Cutting Garden Flowers With Fragrance

**Sweet Pea:** Tender tendrils and abundant blooms make this vining plant perfect for your cutting garden. Watch out, as some varieties do not have scent. Sweet pea grows best on a trellis or some support. This is an annual plant with blossoms in white, lavender and pinks. (Zones 2–11)

**Sweet Autumn Clematis:** Another vine that smells divine! Also known as virgin bower, these starry shaped flowers will send wafts of sweet scent all over your yard. This plant is very hardy and can grow up to twenty-five feet in a season. Sweet autumn clematis is a deciduous vine that can tolerate part shade. Like all clematis, it likes its "feet" is the shade so under plant it with low growers. Late summer to autumn blooming. (Zones 4–11)

**Heliotrope:** Choose the tall variety for your cutting garden. These tropical heat lovers produce small deep violet flowers on branched stems. Heliotropes are annuals. (Zones 2–11)

**Scented Geraniums:** Basic geraniums have a distinct smell, which reminds me of my grandma Sally. She loved the red ones and planted them in container pots made from inverted car tires. Really, she did! Cut open like a bagel and turned inside out, the tires take on the shape of wide squat urns. *Sally was before her time in the chic repurposing department!*

Scented geraniums are actually not geraniums at all. They are pelargoniums. Well, of course they are! The fuzzy leaves of the scented geraniums, not the flowers, are the stars of these plants. The foliage gives off the fabulous and varied fragrance. The plants cool themselves by giving off a wonderful smelling oil from the back of the leaves. *How cool is that!* Scented geraniums are perennials in Zone 8 or above, and annuals where it is colder. (Zones 2–11)

**Dianthus:** Dianthus, also known as sweet william, is an old-fashioned favorite seen in cutting gardens for over a hundred years. These plants flower in pinks, red or white. Dianthus can be annuals, bi annuals or perennials depending on the variety. (Zones 2–11)

**Nicotiana:** Also known as the tobacco plant, nicotiana is an annual, whose flowers unfurl at night. The fragrance is most intoxicating at night in the garden, but will continue in the day light in your house once cut. That being said, if your cutting garden is near a bedroom window, crack it open to enjoy this scent while you sleep before gathering for an arrangement. (Zones 2–11)

**Lavender:** Another plant you will want to smell anytime—but particularly at night—is lavender. Apparently, studies have shown lavender aids in sleep. I must say I agree. For a time I was having trouble staying asleep and a friend suggested I tuck a lavender sachet under my pillow. I did and it definitely helped. Now and again I place a bud vase of lavender sprigs beside my bed: lovely!

Lavender has many different varieties, all of which are perennials above Zone 5. Below Zone 5, lavender is best treated as an annual. (Zones 5–11)

**Rosemary:** Like lavender, rosemary is another herb that should make its way into your cutting garden. Woody and fragrant with a long vase life, rosemary adds a deep green color and an interesting texture, too. It is beautiful juxtaposed with dainty pale pinks and white roses. Rosemary is a perennial, but in colder areas may act like an annual. If you get frost bring your rosemary inside until it warms up again. (Zones 7 –11)

**Mint:** *I know, I know, mint is invasive*, but it is also a fabulous addition to your arrangements and super easy to grow. Plant it in a container that you bury in the ground if you want it to be in the same bed, or in a separate container. Either of those growing methods will allow you to control its spread. There are so many easy-to-grow varieties of mint such as peppermint, chocolate mint, spearmint, and the list goes on. It adds a pop of classic green, a fresh scent, and it has a long vase life. (Zones 2–11)

# CHAPTER TWELVE: BLUE FLOWERS - WHY SO FEW?

In a garden it may not be imperative to have certain colors, but when you are creating a floral bouquet or arrangements for a special event, oftentimes the theme or palette for the occasion demands a certain color. What do you do if that color is blue?

It is said that there is no true blue in the garden, but that isn't really accurate. There are blue flowers, but their numbers are few. Bachelor button, also known as cornflower (which I suggested be planted in your sunny cutting garden), is a true blue. But why so few? Let's learn that answer.

Blue simply does not appear in nature often. Think about it: loads of green, brown, gold and red. White, yellow, pink, and even purple flowers can be found, but hardly any blue. The sky has the market share on blue. Less than 10 percent of 280,000 species of flowering plants produce blue flowers. There are certainly blue-ish flowers, but few true blues.

The answer is simply plants do not have a true blue pigment in them. So the few that turn out true blue had to go through some changes to get there. Worth the effort, I would say!

If you are in the market for some true blue flowers for your own enjoyment or for an event, here are a few to seek out. If planting, keep in mind true blue flowers tend to bloom in early spring or summer.

## THE FEW TRUE BLUES

DELPHINIUMS

BLUE BELLS

MORNING GLORIES

BACHELOR BUTTON/CORNFLOWER

HYDRANGEA

SOME AGAPANTHUS

PLUMBAGO

DAY FLOWER

# CHAPTER THIRTEEN: BEST ROSES FOR ARRANGEMENTS

We cannot talk about floral arranging without mentioning roses. It has been said that roses are one of the only flowers that look better cut, and I agree. Most roses bushes aren't stunning on their own, but the blossoms they produce distract from any lack of beauty in the shrubs.

There are countless roses and each one beautiful enough to simply stand alone in a slim vase. But multiple roses and roses mixed with other flowers take an arrangement to the next level.

Truthfully, I am not a fan of the dozen long-stemmed roses in a vase sort of arrangement. Too much stem and not enough petal for me. That iconic Valentine's Day bouquet is not particularly inspired. Frankly, I don't think the roses, however lovely, are showcased best in this way. I like my roses full, open, lush and tightly packed together for maximum impact.

So, with thousands of roses to choose from, let's explore which are best to grow or buy for floral arranging. I have two words for you with respect to the best roses to grow in your cutting garden: REPEAT BLOOMERS. No one wants their rose bushes to be left bereft of all their beauty after just one or two arrangements. Of course, if you are purchasing instead growing roses for your arrangements, repeat blooming is not a factor you need to consider.

Whether growing or purchasing commercially, choose roses for your arrangements that are in the late bud stage. This stage is characterized by some opened outer petals, but the flower is not fully unfurled. These roses will continue to open in the vase, becoming more beautiful with each passing day.

When choosing roses, look for strong stems and roses that hold their flowers straight up—not bent or those appearing top-heavy. These are signs of poor hydration or damage that will not likely improve. If you find yourself with roses in this condition, you can salvage them by cutting the stem an inch or less from the base of the flower and floating them in a shallow bowl. Once the rose is open enough, it will float and recover enough to be lovely on a nightstand or other area where it can be appreciated up close.

Before we delve into any particular rose, let's take a bit of time to de-mystify roses. This of great importance if you are adding roses to your garden. If you are purchasing flowers for arrangements, it is still wonderful knowledge to have. You can impress or confuse your local flower salesperson by asking, "So you have any pre-1867 roses today?" I'll tell you why.

All the types of roses and the overlapping categories can prove to be truly befuddling. Couple that with the sheer beauty of each one, and you have a recipe for avoidance or mistakes of the "I'll take one of each kind" variety. If you have a solid general understanding of roses and know what type you are looking for, you won't avoid planting roses or be swayed by their charms into planting the wrong ones.

All roses need good soil and lots of sunshine. Thanks to chapter ten you have, or are on the road to having, great soil. Presumably, your cutting garden gets lots of sun, so adding roses is a must. So, let's learn a bit about roses in general, then talk about a few standouts for arrangements.

Roses are generally broken down into three main categories:

WILD ROSES

OLD GARDEN ROSES - PRE 1867

MODERN GARDEN ROSES - POST 1867

For our purposes, we are going to concentrate on the category of modern garden roses. This is not because these roses are necessarily better than wild or old garden roses. In fact, old garden roses are thought to be more disease-proof than their younger counterparts. We are going to focus on modern roses as this category of roses has the most repeat bloomers. And that, my friends, is what we want in our cutting garden.

Modern garden roses in have the hallmarks of a continuous bloom, larger blooms, longer vase life, lack of fragrance, and, as I mentioned, are less hardy and disease resistant. That being said, individual roses in this category defy some of those general characteristics.

I wish I could tell you it was as simple as these three categories, but alas, as with many beautiful things it is more complicated than that. Each of the three main categories is broken down into smaller categories or classes. Let's look at the roses within the modern rose category. These are:

HYBRID TEA

FLORIBUNDA

GRANDIFLORA

POLYANTHA

SHRUB/ENGLISH

CLIMBING

As this is a book on flower arranging, I won't go into detail on these subcategories. I will let you know that shrub, polyantha and grandiflora roses are likely your best bets in the cutting garden for lower maintenance and prolific blooming. Hybrid teas are wonderful cut flowers but are fairly high maintenance.

English roses, a.k.a. the David Austin, are in the shrub category. If you have never looked at the David Austin catalogue, please do. Words cannot describe the beauty on those pages. David Austin Roses have joined the best characteristics of the old garden and modern garden roses. The rosette and fragrance (see, I told you some are scented!) from the old and the repeat flowering and wide range of colors from the modern.

Right about now you might be saying to yourself, "*Kelly, just tell me what rose to grow!*" Okay, but what about color? Oh my... ! Well, here are a few suggestions that would work well in your cutting garden and arrangements. Use these suggestions as a starting point to delve further into the world of roses in the colors your heart desires.

# Some Roses to Consider

HYBRID TEA:       Mr.Lincoln - deep red with rich fragrance

                  Double Delight - pink mixed with yellow

FLORIBUNDA:       Julia Child - buttery yellow

                  French Lace - creamy white mild fruity scent

GRANDIFLORA:      Queen Elizabeth - pink

                  Miss Congeniality - white edged with bright pink

POLYANTHUS:       Cecile Brunner - pale pink to peach

                  Fairy - prolific double pink

SHRUB:            Gertrude Jekyll - pink with strong rose scent

                  Graham Thomas - tall bright yellow mild fruity scent

CLIMBING:         Eden Climber - creamy white/pale pink

                  New Dawn - pale pink

# Chapter Fourteen: WOW Flowers

It is the first of my six essential rules of floral design, after all: Pick a "WOW" flower. Now, this is a rule I can follow every time, and you should too. Every arrangement needs a showstopper: a flower that is just a bit more fabulous than the rest. Keeping the theatrical metaphor going, think of your WOW flowers as the diva/star, the medium sized blooms as the supporting actors, and the small flowers/foliage/grasses as the chorus. There could be no show without all of the players, but the star is essential.

You will have no problem casting your perfect stars. Everyone even remotely interested in flowers has a favorite WOW flower or two. No matter how many WOWs you love, only include one type per arrangement. Specifically, three to five of the same WOW flower in each. There cannot be two types of flower stars in a good design. They will compete, like their human counterparts probably would do.

I am suggesting a few WOW flowers that will last for a while as a cut flower and that work well in arrangements. Maybe one or more of your favorite made the list.

## Suggestions for WOW Flowers

**Peony:** One of the only plants I miss in my Southern California garden. When I gardened in New York, I had the healthiest and most beautiful peonies. Do you know why I cannot have them here? The climate isn't cold enough. I know, hard to feel sorry for me living where I can garden twelve months a year, but I do miss them!

I really do not have to say much other than the word "peony". They are WOW flowers extraordinaire. So, how about I suggest one in particular, festiva maxima. It is a double blossom cultivar to the max!

Peonies like lots of sun, well drained moist soil. As I mentioned they need a cold spell below freezing to bloom. I tried them here and all I got was the tease of beautiful deep green foliage. If you want your peonies to bloom, make sure you are in Zones 3–8.

Whether cutting from the garden or buying commercially, make sure the peonies are about three quarters of the way open. The multitude of petals will continue to unfurl in the arrangement adding to the beauty. The best just keeps getting better!

**Giant White Calla:** From the hundred petals of a peony to none. You see the white curved portion of the calla is not a flower, or even a petal of a flower. It is a leaf. The flower is in the inside. Well, it is technically, but we can think of it as a flower of the WOW variety.

Callas grow from rhizomes, enjoy the full sun, rich sandy soil, and should be kept evenly moist. *Sounds a bit like a diva!* I will let you know, I am going to try this plant in my cutting garden this year. Giant white callas grow to about three feet tall and two feet wide. They bloom in mid spring to summer in Zones 8–10.

**Siberian Iris:** These tall periwinkle colored spires are stunning in an arrangement. In the garden they enjoy full sun, but will tolerate part shade. Keep them evenly moist for best results. With two blooms on each stalk, siberian irises have a long vase life. Cut or purchase when one bloom is three quarters of the way opened or open and the other is still closed.

**Casa Blanca Lilies:** Oh, these beauties are possibly my all-time favorite cut flower. Rock stars in the vase and in the garden, casa blanca lilies steal the show. Outward-facing blooms, highly fragrant with a heady scent, plays well with others or can stand alone, these flowers should be on your short list too.

In the garden, casa blancas are grown from bulbs. They enjoy full sun on their faces and cool soil at their feet. So, plant these bulbs where the sun shines for six to eight hours and underplant with low growing plants at the base of the lilies to provide shade. The soil needs to be well draining and the bulbs planted at a depth of three times the size of the bulb.

When cutting from the garden for an arrangement, take care to leave as much stem as possible. Cut only about one third, leaving enough leaves on the remaining stem to feed the bulb for the coming year. Cut the stem on an angle and follow my advice for lasting cut flowers.

When purchasing casa blanca lilies, choose stems with buds just about to open. You will see the white showing through. Do not choose stems with only tight green buds. Even if some of the flowers are open, it is fine as these lilies have many buds per stem. Remove the anthers (which carry the pollen) to avoid it dropping onto the crisp white petals or your clothes. With the proper care I have educated you on, casa blanca lilies can last up to two weeks in a container. Told you they were rock stars!

**Gerber Daisies:** You say gerbera, I say gerber. A gerber by any other spelling is still a WOW flower! These daisies are so vibrant they can't help but make a statement in any design. Gerber daisies might just be the happiest looking flowers.

Gerber daisies can be grown from seed, but it is difficult and you cannot be sure which variety will end up in your garden. Better methods are from seedling, divided plant, or transplanted potted plant.

Gerbers need full sun, sandy soil, and a bit of compost at planting to thrive. Plant gerbers with the crown visible. If they are planted too deeply they will likely suffer from crown rot. Let the crown dry out between waterings.

Display gerbers in vase with only other gerbers, or better yet, one stem each in many vases. Add only an inch of water. A large volume of shallow water is ideal for lasting blooms. Gerbers like to be alone because they soak up a lot of water if given the chance. In fact, they almost drown themselves, resulting in weak stems. Weak stems equal faded flowers. Make the stems work a little harder by giving them less water to soak up and they will stay strong to support the glorious blossoms. You can also snip off the ends when you see them getting soggy.

You can mix gerbers in with other flowers, but keep the water level shallow and replenish often. These water hogs will drink it all up and the others will go thirsty. For a low maintenance gerber arrangements, pop one or two in three vases of differing heights and cluster the vases together.

With the stunning color of gerbers, one in a vase is plenty. Scatter the vases around your whole house for a bit of cheer everywhere. These particular daisies are no 'wallflowers' so have no problem going it alone. Follow my advice and your gerbers will last and last.

**Tulips:** Tulips are grown from bulbs. They are planted in the fall and blossom in the spring. Cold winters and dry summers are the ticket for healthy happy tulips. Tulips prefer full sun, sandy soil and little moisture.

Dig holes (or a trench 8 inches deep), spacing the bulbs four to six inches apart. Plant tips up, then cover, pat and water. After the initial watering, do not water again. Tulip bulbs are perennials, coming back year after year in colder climates.

Where it gets cold, plant the bulbs 6 weeks before the hard frost. If treating them as perennials, feed when you plant. In warmer climates, tulip bulbs need to be stored in the refrigerator for several weeks before planting to give them the cold snap they need. Then, plant when it is below 60 degrees. Plant lots and lots of tulips in the fall, so you have plenty for spring bouquets.

Like most bulbs, if planted correctly tulips will, well...just grow! See how easy that is? Once the flowers have faded, deadhead. Let the foliage yellow for about 6 weeks after the flower has faded. Then you can clear it away. Water sparingly throughout the growing season. Tulips dislike too much moisture.

If you live where it is cold, just leave the tulips in the garden. In warmer climates you can dig up the bulbs and store in a cool dry place until a few weeks before planting. At that time, pop them back in the refrigerator until temps are below 60 degrees. Then take them out and plant. Or just start again with new bulbs in the fall.

Tulips are a perfect cut flower. To have your bouquets look their best and last longer, re-cut the stems under water. Place immediately in cool water—not ice water. Cut the stem straight across as with other hollow-stemmed flowers. As mentioned, despite the fact that they are both iconic spring flowers, don't mix daffodils or other narcissus flowers with your tulips. Remember: daffodils give off a toxic sap.

Tulips are extraordinary cut flowers in that their stems continue to grow even after being cut: up to an inch or more! Another interesting characteristic of tulips is they are phototropic. This means they bend toward the light. Hence, rotate your vase if you notice them bending to the light source. I think I am phototropic too, are you?

# CHAPTER FIFTEEN - WHERE TO PURCHASE FLOWERS

No cutting garden? No worries! You can pick up lovely flowers at your local grocery shop, farmer's market, head to a flower mart, or buy flowers online. If you are not sure if you have a flower mart in your city or town, here is a list of the marts I know exist. I suggest googling "flower mart (insert closest city)" to find out if there is one near you.

## UNITED STATES FLOWER MARTS

CHICAGO

LOS ANGELES

NEW YORK

OKLAHOMA

PHOENIX

SAN FRANCISCO

SEATTLE

I frequent the Los Angeles Flower Market (L.A. Flower Mart). It is vast, a world unto itself, and it has every flower and floral accessory/supply you can think of within its walls. And know what else? It is cheap and sells wholesale to the public. The public in the know that is - *now you are part of that knowledgeable public.*

The L.A. Flower Mart started over a century ago when flower growers drove their blooms by horse and carriage to a central downtown location for sale to florists and other merchants. Two markets arose from this trade: the European and the Japanese. This was circa 1916.

As the desire for fresh flowers grew, so did the markets. Housed across the street from each other in downtown L.A. the Marts operate a brisk business six days a week. Today, the L.A. Flower Mart is the largest wholesale flower distributor in the United States, and my playground!

You can stroll in, pay a $2.00 fee, and feast your eyes on bloom after bloom. Sometimes, you walk in an entrance and no one is even there to collect the modest fee. If you are a florist, dealer or other such wholesaler, you can walk right in as soon as the Mart opens, which is 2 a.m. on certain days. The public—me and you—can walk at 8 a.m. *A much more civilized hour.* But don't show up much later than that, as the market doesn't stay open all day.

On trips to the Flower Mart, I usually bring along my "old lady cart", as my daughter calls it: a red wire rolling cart on wheels to hold my bouquets and supplies. Let's face it, getting carried away in the flower mart is easy, but carrying it all to the car is not! Hence, the cart.

If you are heading to a mart near you, I suggest doing the same, or be ready to exert some powerful self control. At about one-third the retail price and with the overwhelming selection, I venture to say your arms will overflow too! Bring a cart and bring a plan. It is good to arrive at a mart with a plan. Without one, you'll drift along from vendor to vendor wanting one of everything. F-O-C-U-S! Despite all the attractive distractions.

The L.A. Flower Mart, (as well as the New York Mart), is pretty loose-y goose-y about public times, entrance fees, and letting the non-credentialed visitors pay with credit cards. I understand other U.S. flower marts are stricter. I have never been stopped while walking in the L.A. Mart even before eight a.m., never been asked for my "papers" (credentials), nor was my credit card ever not accepted. All this being said, best practice is to arrive when the public is allowed, pay your fee, and purchase with cash. I prefer to pay in cash at the Mart anyway, as a means of self-control. When I run out of greenbacks, it is time to head home. A credit card can be dangerous!

I am thinking about all these flower markets and conjuring up a dream trip. A visit to all of the major U.S. flower marts! Should we plan a field trip? And, then there is Europe to explore! *Be still my beating heart!* Until we can organize such an outing, let's explore buying flowers online.

If you don't live near a flower mart and you are not satisfied with the selection at your local shops, you can purchase fresh flowers online. It is not as crazy as its sounds. Think about it: florists get most (if not all) of their flowers shipped to them.

If you buy flowers online from a reputable grower or supplier they will give you instructions on how to best rehydrate the particular blooms you purchased. In most (if not all) cases, you will follow the same advice I have provided you with here. Buying flowers online opens up a world or shall I say *garden* of choices. If you are in need a certain flower for an occasion or just want to treat yourself to your favorites that you cannot find nearby, give online cut flowers a try.

# CHAPTER SIXTEEN: FLORAL DESIGNING SUPPLIES

Let's look at the list of floral supplies I suggest, then cover each one in more depth as necessary. There are, of course, countless other floral designing supplies for very specific purposes. My list consists of what you need to make all the arrangements in the book and many, many others. These are the basic supplies to have on hand to whip up an arrangement when the mood strikes you.

## Floral Supplies

- Floral shears

- Floral foam

- Clear adhesive tape

- Wired sticks

- Chopsticks

- Wire

- Jars / containers

- Pebbles

- Moss

- Plastic bucket

## Floral Shears:

I am not one for a lot of supplies and gadgets. For example, in the kitchen, I forgo the specialized tools for a sharp all-purpose knife. That and your hands will get most jobs done well. That being said, sometimes a special tool not only gets the job done well, but done more easily. This is the case with floral shears and flower arranging.

A sharp knife works perfectly well to trim stems, but floral shears do as good a job and are easier for most people to work with, especially for underwater cuts. The reason floral shears work better for cutting flowers than regular scissors is because floral shears are designed to avoid crushing the flower stems. A crushed stem prevents water from reaching the flower head and results in drooping arrangements. Using floral shears to cut stems gives your flowers the best chance of long term survival in the arrangements you create. Well worth the approximately twenty dollar investment.

In choosing floral shears, look for ones that are have medium-length blades made of a non-rusting material. Try them out (if possible) to make sure your hand can fit comfortably. If buying online, read the reviews to assess the grip.

## Floral Foam:

Floral foam is a great help in getting flowers to stay put, especially in shallow containers. It is lightweight and made of resins, which inhibit the growth of bacteria. The other feature of floral foam is that it soaks up lots of water, keeping flowers hydrated. The most common floral foam is made by Oasis, but any floral foam will do.

Floral foam comes in many shapes and sizes. For container arrangements, the simple rectangular bricks are best suited. Floral foam can be cut with a sharp knife to fit the container. Once wet, you can even mold it into a desired shape.

To prepare foam for a container arrangement, fill a sink, basin or bucket with water to cover the foam completely. You need only let it sit for a minute or two to be fully hydrated. Make sure the foam was fully submerged so there aren't any dry spots. Remove from the water and place in the container. Once the foam is in the container, fill with additional water for the flowers. While the foam provides some hydration, it is not a replacement for clean water. The main purpose of the foam is to allow you to add flowers and heavy berries or fruits to an arrangement to achieve a beautiful and professional looking design.

## Clear Adhesive Tape:

The purpose of the tape is to create a grid over the opening of a container into which you slip your flowers. Adhesive tape in floral design has basically the same purpose as the foam: to keep your flowers in the spot you want them, helping you to create flow in your design. As with the foam, the tape is most useful in shallow wide-mouth containers wherein the stems have to be cut short and the flowers have no other anchor.

## Florists Tape:

This tape is strong and bonds to wet or dry material. It is used primarily to hold wet foam in place.

## Wired Sticks:

When I say "wired stick", I am talking about the green pointed sticks with the bit of copper wire attached to one end. These are used to firm up wimpy stems when you are using foam or pebbles to sure up an arrangement.

To use a wired stick, cut the flower stem to the desired length. While holding the stick (with the point in line with the bottom of the stem), twirl the wire around the stem and stick from the top of the stick to the bottom of the stem. Joining the stick with the stem will make it make sturdier when you insert it into the foam or pebbles.

## Chopsticks:

I use chopsticks or wooden skewers to hold fruit in my arrangements and to firm up longer or weaker stems. I wrap wire around the stick/skewer and the stem, starting from the top of the stick/skewer and moving down to bottom of the stem. In a pinch, you can even use a real stick or long cut sturdy stem from another flower to serve the same purpose of the chopsticks or skewers. Only do this in a pinch, though, as the real stick or stem may carry some bacteria.

Chopsticks are also useful to make holes in your foam for weak-stemmed flowers that wouldn't be able to push through. Push the chopstick in and make a guide hole for the wimpy stems to slide into without resistance.

## Wire:

As mentioned above, I use wire to wrap stems with sturdy sticks. Wire can also be used to secure flowers in small containers. Bunch up some wire into a loose ball to fit your small container. The stems of your flowers can slide between the wire and rest on others. While not as exacting as inserting flowers into foam, wire can help keep the design in place.

## Jars / Containers:

I have never seen a jar I didn't like: just so much potential for repurposing and so useful. I regularly take the time to remove labels and thoroughly clean jars of sauce, jam or other foods. The more interesting the shape, the better. You can clean them up and leave as-is or spray paint, roll in glitter, glue on leaves: *see, so much potential!*

Along with my stash of clean jars, I collect thrifted containers for my floral designs. Even if the piece does not suit my decor, if it is pretty or interesting I grab it for events or to give to friends filled with flowers. If you are creating arrangements for an event and need several, check out your local dollar store for inexpensive plastic matching containers. Nondescript plastic containers in neutral colors can be hidden by flowers, ivy, or other soft flowing plant materials for those arrangements.

## Moss:

Moss can make an appearance in topiary or other types of arrangements wherein the flowers are rising out of the vase. We will use moss in such an arrangement when we reach the month of April's tutorial. Moss is also perfect to soften or blur the edge of a container.

## Pebbles:

Along with foam and balled up wire, pebbles can be used to form a base in the container. A few inches of pebbles will hold the flowers securely in place. It is a good idea to toss a few handfuls of pebbles in any container that might be unsteady due to top-heavy blooms. Giving a bit of ballast to an arrangement is always a good idea if you are concerned it will topple over. Do make sure the pebbles are clean; you do not want to introduce any dirt or bacteria to your beautiful creation.

## Plastic Bucket:

A plastic bucket or a large vase is useful to hold the flowers not only while they are re-hydrating, but also while you are working on the arrangement. Leaving flowers out of water for even a few minutes can significantly shorten their life span. Design with a "working bucket" and the actual container, taking flowers from one and immediately placing in the other.

# Chapter Seventeen: Design

Classic design, modern design - YOUR design. In floral design the beauty is truly in the eye of the beholder and the creator. Thus far in this book, I have shared with you principles, rules, practical advice, and tips on how to select, grow, and cut flowers, as well as how best to preserve floral arrangements. Now, we get to the less concrete and more interpretive section of the book. You know how to choose, grow, and care for your flowers. Now it is time to get creative!

Armed with the knowledge of what I shared in the previous chapters, you are more than ready to let YOUR creative energies flow into gorgeous floral designs that express you, your home and/or your event.

Unleash your imagination and let's have some fun creating twelve arrangements together: one for each month of the year. Replicate each one or use as a springboard from which your designs can *stem.* (Sorry, couldn't resist the pun!)

When starting any arrangement, choose your flowers and container. Grab any supplies you might need and make sure everything is super clean. Find a pleasant place to work (*can we even call this work?*) and create!

Although each of the twelve designs we do together will be different, you will follow the same simple steps. This will be true of every arrangement you ever make. So, remember the practical information that came before, or refer back to the previous chapters.

Keep my six essential rules of floral design particularly in mind (see Chapter Four if you need a refresher) as we delve into each arrangement and do the following four things in the following order for each mixed design:

1. Start with greens, making a framework for the arrangement.

2. Add small to medium flowers in balance

3. Tuck in the WOW flowers

4. Nestle in fill flowers, berries or other accents

Not only easy, but also relaxing and fun! I have a couple of additional thoughts for you to keep in mind before we begin:

Negative space is a good thing in design, and add flowers on an angle. Negative space gives the eye a place to rest. Bald spots, on the other hand, are not good. Make sure to walk around or turn your arrangement around now and again as you are working on it so you can fill in where it may look sparse. When adding the flowers to a mixed arrangement, angle them into the container. Do not stick them in straight up like soldiers. Angling will give your designs a lovely shape.

Each of the next chapters will be month by month, starting with January, naturally. First, we'll talk a bit about the arrangement. I will list the flowers and supplies needed. Then we'll dive into the tutorial, followed by a few design-specific tips. Okay, *ready*? Let's get started...

*"People from a planet without flowers would think we would be mad with joy the whole time to have such things about us."*

Iris Murdoch

# January

In January, I am ready for a clean sweep of all the beautiful abundance that is the holidays. The end of the annual celebrations coupled with the dawn of a new year makes all the world seem ready for freshness. In my home, that means a deep clean. In my work, a crisp new planner. In my mind, thoughts of new ventures and best intentions to do more sit-ups! In my florals, January means white. Clean, textured, fragrant, all-white flowers overflow my vases.

Having fresh, fragrant flowers in the house in January fills the void that putting away all the decorations creates. Since a tree or other holiday decor can be pretty big, I like to replace it with a big arrangement on my dining room table. So, let's kick off the year with an extra-large arrangement, shall we? What is the saying "Go big or go home"? Well, for us, now it is, "Go BIG at home!"

## JANUARY FLOWERS AND SUPPLIES:

- Casa blanca lilies or crystal blanca lilies

- Genestra stems

- Tall, clear glass vase (or urn)

- Several feet of large link chain from the hardware store

# January Tutorial

**1**  Fill the vase/urn one third of the way with treated water.

**2**  Encircle the chain in the bottom of the urn.

**3**  Keeping your lily stems long, start inserting the stems into the chain links, crossing them as you insert and keeping the stems together in the center.

**4**  Slip in the long wispy stems of genestra around the edges and one in the middle and one in the front and let it flop over. Casual elegance at its floral best!

# January Tips

Lilies are heavy flowers, so they need an anchor in a vase, especially if you are leaving the stems long as I did for our January arrangement. I came up with the chain idea as a stylish way to anchor the stems. If you choose not to join my chain gang, just make sure you have something in the bottom of the vase, such as glass pebbles or rocks. I was considering using rocks spray-painted gold before landing on the chain idea. However, rocks and pebbles can block the end of the stems. I like the chain not only for the look, but also the open links let you insert and anchor the stems without blocking the water supply. I used 30 feet of chain in this vase.

Casa blanca lilies are fabulous, but so are crystal blanca lilies. To the eye, there is virtually no difference. To the nose, casa blancas have a stronger scent. However, the crystal blancas have stronger stems, and they are less expensive. These 20 stems of crystal blancas set me back only $20 at the flower market. The casa blancas would have been $25 for 15 stems. *Can you believe $20 for all these lilies?!*

When arranging with lilies, remove the stamens from the flowers before the pollen appears. Get to them right as they are opening. I use my floral shears to gently pluck the stamen off at the tip. It is kind of like playing that old board game Operation. You need a steady hand or *bam*! the stamen stains the petal. If so, just blow it off. As a precaution I also suggest holding a paper towel under the flower you are 'operating' on in case a pollen-y stamen falls. No need to stain your tablecloth or clothes. Catch the stamen early enough, before the pollen has emerged, and you are safe from stains.

*"If I had a flower for every time I thought of you, I could walk through my garden forever."*

Alfred Lord Tennyson

# FEBRUARY

I can't help but think of Valentine's Day when the calendar flips to February. Even if there isn't a Cupid in sight, we all deserve a bouquet this time of year. Midwinter may have you closed up inside, either by the cold or with a cold, and flowers are the cure for either.

I said the silliest thing to my husband years ago: "Don't get me flowers for Valentine's Day." What I really meant and meant to say was, "Don't get me one of those uninspired, overpriced, cliché arrangements for Valentine's Day." Well, let's just say the distinction was lost and I don't get flowers on Valentine's Day. Whether you do or you don't, make this sweet design for yourself or your valentine. It is decidedly inspired, inexpensive, and unique.

## February: Flowers and Supplies

- Red tulips

- White spray roses

- Boxwood or other deep green foliage

- Budding cherry laurel or other tiny white flower in bud

- A vintage or valentine tin

- Drinking glass or tall jar

# FEBRUARY TUTORIAL

1   Find a vintage or unique tin and a glass/jar that will fit inside it.

2   Fill the glass or jar with treated water and slide into the tin.

3   Pinprick the tulips to release any trapped air in the stem.

4   Add in the greens, splaying out from the center, thereby creating a framework for the other flowers.

5   Add in the spray roses on an angle and in clumps

6   Insert the tulips. A bunch of five or so is perfect.

7   Fill in with sprigs of tiny white flowers to soften the design. Pay particular attention to softening the edge with these flowers and the roses.

# February Tips

When inserting the greens and flowers in an arrangement that has a container within a container, make sure that the stems are making it into the inner container filled with water.

Even if your tulips aren't droopy, it doesn't hurt to give them a precautionary pinprick in case there is some air trapped in the stem. Insert the pin at the top of the stem nearest to where it meets the flower head.

Re-cut your tulips in a few days, as they will continue to grow in the arrangement.

Look for greens and tiny buds in your garden. Even in the dead of winter, evergreen trees will give you a few stems and maybe a few buds. Just stay away from pine or holly. Coupled with the red, those greens will give the design a decidedly Christmas vibe. Keep in mind for Christmas though, as holiday tins are easy to come by at thrift stores and flea markets.

*"In joy or sadness, flowers are our constant friends."*

Kakuzo Okakura

# MARCH

In case you can't locate a vintage tin such as the one I used for February's design, I wanted you to share a tutorial using a tin most everyone can find at their local market.

So for March we have golden yellow roses, green berries, and boxwood in a McCann's Oatmeal tin. This vintage-looking tin is probably sitting right on the shelf in the cereal aisle of your favorite grocery store. Go get one!

As with the vintage tin, slide in a glass or jar containing treated water. The McCann's tin will be waterproof so you can go without, but I think the insert helps the flowers stay put. The tin has a fairly wide opening. A small Mason jar fits perfectly inside a McCann's tin and closes the width of the opening just enough to better support the stems. You could also make a grid with adhesive tape to keep the flowers in place, but I think the inner jar is easier to work with in a tight space.

To soften the edge of the tin and add texture, I have included burlap ribbon. You can cut a square of burlap or two strips of wide burlap ribbon to achieve the same look. I think a black and white checked pattern might be darling as well. Even a checked napkin would do if it is on the small side. Too much material looks sloppy— you just want a bit peeking out.

# March - Flowers and Supplies

- Golden yellow spray roses

- Green coffee bean berries

- Boxwood or another deep green foliage

- A McCann's oatmeal tin

- A small Mason jar

- Burlap fabric: in a 16 inch square, or two 16 inch long strips of wide (6 inch) burlap ribbon

# MARCH TUTORIAL

**1** Cut the burlap or ribbon. If you are using ribbon, once you cut the two 16 inch strips, cross them over each other to form an X.

**2** Place the burlap or X of ribbon centered on the opening of the oatmeal tin.

**3** Fill the Mason jar with treated water and slip it into the tin, pushing the burlap into the opening. The burlap/ribbon will overlap the edge of the tin. You can trim to suit after the flowers are in, if necessary.

**4** Start (as always with) a base of greens for foundation. If the foliage has more than a few branches to it, three stems should suffice.

**5** Add in the spray roses. Place the tallest in the center. Angle in the other rose stems using the greenery as the anchor.

**6** Intersperse clusters of green coffee bean berries throughout the arrangement creating flow and adding more texture. Coffee bean berries are a terrific choice for cut arrangements. They are inexpensive, long lasting (10 to 21 days) and come in a range of colors. As such, we will use them in red, white, and green in a few of our arrangements.

**7** As with all floral designs, rotate the container or walk around it to make sure the back side looks as good as the front.

**8** Fluff the burlap if necessary, and allow some roses and greenery to nestle into the fabric.

# MARCH TIPS

Leave the shorter stemmed spray roses on the main stem. Tucking the stems in with these shorter stemmed blooms creates instant depth.

Clusters of berries may mean more than one stem. It looks better to have fewer clusters of more berries, than more single stem berries all over the arrangement.

As with all double container arrangements, make sure the stems are in the water.

*"You must be an angel since you care for flowers."*

Victor Hugo

# APRIL

April's design is a bit of a departure for me. I rarely design single bloom arrangements and prefer a loose look rather than a linear one. That being said, daffodils are loners. Or, should be loners *and* I wanted to show you how to use a flower frog.

So April is a daffodil topiary with moss. I think it is oh so very springy! Small faux Easter eggs or chocolate eggs could be scattered amongst the moss for a lovely holiday centerpiece. Even though it is tall, it is narrow enough not to be awkward on the dining table during a meal.

# April Flowers and Supplies

- Two bunches of daffodils

- Green moss

- A lidless tureen or large bowl

- Adhesive tape (double sided is best)

- Large flower frog

- Ribbon or twine

# April Tutorial

**1**  Place flower frog in the tureen or bowl.

**2**  Mix up water and preservative. Pour the treated water over the frog so it is covered by two to three inches of water, but that the water isn't up to the rim.

**3**  Grasp the daffodils in your hand loosely and arrange so that the outer flowers are facing out and the stems are lined up.

**4**  Once arranged in your hand, grasp a bit tighter and wrap a piece of double sided tape around the stems about two thirds of the way down.

**5**  Turn the taped bouquet so the stems bottoms are facing the frog. With your eye, center the stems on the frog and with a swift purposeful motion, insert the stems into the frog.

**6**  Let go of the flowers and they should stay erect. You may even be surprised at how sturdy they are in the frog. Frogs really work!

**7**  Take the tape and make a lattice type grid over the top of the container. This will form the "bed" for the moss.

**8**  Tuck the moss around the stems and work out to the edges, letting some moss flow over the edge a bit. This will soften the look.

**9**  Wrap a ribbon or twine around the tape on the stems. You can make a lovely bow or go simple, as I did.

# APRIL TIPS

DO NOT recut the daffodils! Remember: they give off a sap, which may block the water from getting to the flower head. If you recut, you are opening up the stem bottom again and would have to re-condition the flowers.

Look for lidless tureens at yard sales. You can often get them for a few dollars. Tureens are wonderful for all sorts of arrangements. As they are wide, you will need foam, or a frog as we used here.

As I mentioned earlier on, be generally aware of the recommended height for a centerpiece on a dining table when designing. A short one should be 12 inches or under, and a tall one 24 inches or higher. This way, neither will block the view across the table.

*"Perfumes are the feelings of flowers."*

Heinrich Heine

# MAY

May's design is bursting with lush and lovely petals. Peonies, ranunculus, roses, and tulips overflow in the vase. I think this arrangement is what the rhymer contemplated when he or she penned, "April showers bring May flowers". Well worth the wait.

I chose peonies as the WOW flower in this design. For me, peonies are the ones that got away (or maybe the ones that stayed behind). I had the most gorgeous healthy peonies in my Southampton NY garden. Alas, here in Southern California, they do not grow. Peonies need really cold weather in the dormant winter to bloom in the spring. So, this is a design is a reminiscence for me.

Peonies would look beautiful in a plastic cup, but for this special arrangement, I chose to use a Bavarian hand-painted pitcher that I picked up at an estate sale. It is quite lovely and compliments the flowers so well. The hand-painted flowers almost seem part of the arrangement.

You can find similar hand-painted floral vases, pitchers, and other china pieces for a song at yard sales, thrift stores, and antique shops. These fragile works of art are not so in vogue right now, but are perfect as an accent or as a compliment to lush arrangements like this one. This pitcher only set me back $10 and has repaid that hundreds of times with the beauty it adds to my florals.

For this arrangement, I used foam to hold the lush flowers in place. I am not opposed to foam, I just generally prefer the looser look achieved by simply using water in a container. However, with these particular flowers and the wide opening of my pitcher, I decided foam would be a good idea. The flowers would give me a loose look by their nature as they continue to open, but would stay in place with the foam. The best of both worlds collide sometimes!

# MAY FLOWERS AND SUPPLIES

- 5 pink peonies

- One bunch pink ranunculus (8-10 stems)

- 5 purple tulips

- White spray roses

- Boxwood greens

- Floral foam

# MAY TUTORIAL

**1** Cut foam and wedge into the container.

**2** Add treated water and let sit a few minutes to absorb. Add more water if needed.

**3** Create a framework with your greens. Use greens sparingly in this design—the greens here are really only for a bit of structure and to create resting spots for the eye. The flowers are the stars.

**4** Tuck in the spray roses on an angle to create instant depth.

**5** Add in the ranunculus in clusters of three.

**6** Pinprick the tulips and arrange singularly throughout.

**7** Lastly, place the 5 peonies throughout the design. Keep in mind that they will open further as the days pass, so give them a bit of room to shine.

# MAY TIPS

It is best to buy, cut, and work with peonies when most of the buds are closed, but soft to the touch, like marshmallows. This indicates they are on the verge of opening so they will improve over time in your arrangement.

A few closed buds in a design add to the natural charm. So, don't fret if one or two never open.

When arranging with peonies for an event, create the design a few days ahead to allow for full effect of the blooms. Therefore, choose companion flowers that have a long vase life (like spray roses) and those that will improve in 24–48 hours, such as ranunculus and tulips. (Ahhh...my choices are not just random beauties!)

For an arrangement using foam, floral tape is a good thing to have on hand if the foam cannot be wedged tightly into the container.

To refresh water using foam, simply hold the foam with a finger or two while tilting and pouring the water out. Refill with a pitcher or measuring cup filled with treated water cover the foam by two to three inches.

As you learned earlier in a previous chapter, tulips will continue to grow in an arrangement. So, one morning you may wake to find them poking out further than you like. Simply pull out gently, trim the stem, and reposition. They will benefit from the fresh cut anyway.

*"Just living is not enough. One must have sunshine, freedom and a little flower."*

Hans Christian Andersen

# JUNE

What a lovely month June is. Summer has just begun, school is out and nature is at a crescendo. It is also a month for lots of garden parties, graduations, and weddings. Let's mark this month with a darling little design that has personality enough to hold its own at a big soiree, yet is small enough to delight and fit on a table for two. Our June floral arrangement is in a vintage teacup.

# June Flowers and Supplies

- Frilly tulips

- Small or tiny round flowers (like feverfew)

- Wispy filler flowers (like wax flower )

- Short sprigs of greenery

- Moss

- Thrifted teacups

- Floral foam

# June Tutorial

**1** Thrift or (dig out from a cupboard) a vintage teacup and saucer.

**2** Cut a small, thin piece of foam to wedge in the cup. Hold in pace with florist tape if necessary.

**3** Fill the cup with treated water.

**4** Follow all the rules for creating a large arrangement (creating flow, vary size, use texture and include a WOW flower): just do it on a small/tiny scale.

**5** Start with the greens for the foundation. Not too much though—you need room for the rest.

**6** Slide the small flowers into the foam, creating a tight dome effect over the top of the cup.

**7** Add in the tulips: 3 or 4 works well.

**8** Tuck in clusters of the tiny wispy flowers in between the tulips.

**9** Nestle in the moss under the flowers and let it drip off the edge of the cup for a softer look.

## June Tips

As this is a tiny arrangement, choose flowers that will not overpower when fully opened. This is the only occasion I can think of that peonies would not be a good choice. I like tulips in teacup designs. Even when the tulips are fully opened, many are more upright and oval in shape. Round flowers on the small side would be good choices too, like marigolds.

Overall, your flower choices for this petite design should be medium/small, to tiny to wispy. In the "wispy" department, don't turn your nose up to baby's breath. I agree it is a bit trite in larger arrangements, but is perfectly suited for a sweet little cuppa joy like this design.

Water may dry up quickly as there isn't much that can fit in the container—so check often and replenish with fresh treated water when needed.

*"A flower blossoms for its own joy."*

Oscar Wilde

# JULY

We can all take a cue from July's quote and blossom for our own joy! This month's design does just that and more. It seems to burst forth and almost explode. *You see where I am going with this?*

I think that "Miss July" looks like the floral version of fireworks. The red hot kalanchoe, rocket shaped muscari, sprightly snowball feverfew, and star shaped sea holly look like the fireworks that splay open in the sky.

Shape, color, and form of flowers and the vessel that holds them can subtly, yet surely, suggest a theme, occasion or feeling. July is a good example of this. There is no flag stuck in the foam, but the choice and combination of flowers tell a story, if you will. Think of this as you design any arrangement and use flower choice and color to convey your message.

# July Flowers and Supplies

- Kalonchoe

- Sea holly

- Muscari a.k.a. grape hyacinth

- Snowball feverfew

- Floral foam

- Small galvanized pail

- Chopstick

- Sparkler (optional)

# JULY TUTORIAL

**1** Wedge the foam inside the pail. I am using foam as the kalanchoe has a short stem and is top heavy.

**2** Fill the pail with treated water to 2–3 inches over the top of the foam.

**3** Start this design with the sea holly. It will act as foundation and mid-sized flower.

**4** Add in three tufts of kalanchoe.

**5** Tuck in 3–5 muscari grouped together for best effect. Let them stand at different heights, which adds to the launching rocket feel.

**6** Gently gather five to seven snowball feverfew together. They have very thin stems. As such, you may want to wire them with the green stick/wire. Or you can try what I did here: use the chopstick to make a hole in the foam and slip the group of stems into the pre-made hole.

**7** Let the snowballs rise above and sink below, creating depth and also giving the sense of exploding forth from the arrangement.

**8** My final step was the circle the rim with sea holly. I like the way that blurs the edge of the pail and creates a necklace around the design.

# JULY TIPS

Make three of these to set down on the center of an outdoor dining table. Add a sparkler to each. Have friends over to celebrate the 4th of July, Bastille Day, or any summer night. Give 3 people long matches and tell them to light the sparklers at the same time. As the sparklers begin to glow, toast to the summer! It will only last a few moments, but will be memorable all the same.

Kalanchoe is an unusual as a cut flower, but is a wonderful choice. It is a succulent known for being a carefree houseplant. It is also a carefree cut flower that lasts and lasts. It has antiseptic properties that actually keep the water crystal clear.

This arrangement will be very long lasting. At least 10 - 15 days. The sea holly and kalanchoe will further out last the muscari and snowballs in a container. To keep the arrangement going even longer, simply pull out and/or place any of the snowballs and muscari as they fade. As always, refresh and replenish the water. Doing this could keep your arrangement going for two weeks or more.

*"I perhaps owe having become a painter to flowers."*

Claude Monet

# AUGUST

The sun and water of summer come together in our August arrangement. The heat of the sun is reflected in the monochromatic orange flower palette. The water is represented by the cobalt blue of the bowl.

The design is a loose triangle with openness. Keep that in mind as you add your flowers. For greatest impact, I forewent greenery besides the leaves on the flowers themselves. The structure comes from the sturdier stemmed flowers such as the snapdragons and dahlias. This arrangement shows the power of a single color arrangement.

# August Flowers and Supplies

- Orange dahlias

- Orange ranunculus

- Orange spray roses

- Burnt orange alstromeria

- Orange/salmon snapdragons

- 10–12 inch wide shallow bowl

- Large piece of floral foam

- Florist's tape

# August Tutorial

1 Cut foam to fit the bowl as best you can, and tape it in place with a grid pattern.

2 Fill with treated water to soak the foam and then add a bit more, but not up to the lip of the bowl yet.

3 As there is no additional greenery, the foam will give the foundation and the snapdragons will lend the structure.

4 As we are creating a wide triangle rising out of the bowl, two-thirds or more of the design will be flowers.

5 Trim the snapdragons tall: you can always cut them a bit more, but you can't get the height back.

6 Insert three snapdragons of graduated heights in the center of the foam/bowl. These will mark the top of the triangle. All the other flowers will flow down and out from these.

7 To mark the width of the triangle, insert four snapdragons at a severe angle to the sides at equal intervals around the edge of the bowl. These stems should point gently upward, not straight out to the sides.

8 Add in the spray roses. Start with a stem up near the snapdragons. Then, work your way around the arrangement, inserting the roses into the foam in a loose triangle.

9 Now add in the dahlias. Again, start with one near the apex and work around and down the arrangement. Push a few further in to create depth.

10 Circle the edge of the bowl with alstroemeria, almost at a 90-degree angle to the foam. You want it to fill and soften the lip of the bowl, so it should be hanging over the rim.

11 Fill in with the very vibrant orange ranunculus all around the design. Add these in groups of three or five for best results.

12 Finally, find the perfect spot to showcase your design and then fill to the brim with treated water. Shallow bowls are hard to move filled with water, so best to pour it once in place. The resting spot should stay out of direct light as with all cut flower arrangements.

## August Tips

Don't try to get away with regular tape to hold down the foam. It will appear like it is working, then when you are almost done, it will spring away from the edge and your foam will float. Your flowers with be passengers on an unmoored boat floating around the bowl. To stay tethered use waterproof florist's tape.

Check the water level often, as the bowl is shallow and the foam will soak much of it up.

Trim snapdragons as necessary. They may straighten up after being cut and all the hydration. You may want to shorten them a bit in a day or so if they are standing too tall.

*"Weeds are flowers too."*

Eyore / A.A. Milne

# SEPTEMBER

By no means is our September bouquet a bunch of weeds. But what constitutes a weed is up for argument, or at least interpretation. Like all else in life, whether something is a weed or a flower is all in the way you look at it. We have astilbe in this design. There are plenty of plants growing that have the same look as astilbe, but are considered weeds. Let's open our minds and our vases to the possibility that the weeds we encounter are simple flowers waiting to be looked upon with the right eyes.

When I think of September, I believe I will always think of back to school—whether my own return or that of my girls. I venture to say even later on in my life I will have the lingering sense of a new beginning mid-calendar. With new beginnings come new friends, new teachers, and opportunities to make someone feel special. Our September arrangement does that in the simplest way, with a Mason jar filled with flowers.

# SEPTEMBER FLOWERS AND SUPPLIES

- Astilbe

- White spray roses

- Muscari a.k.a. grape hyacinth

- White coffee bean berries

- Sea holly

- Small Mason jar or any other clear jar

# September Tutorial

**1** Fill the jar with treated water.

**2** Place the flowers in separate piles in front of you.

**3** You will build the arrangement in your hand, so place the stems in one palm and hold loosely.

**4** Build the arrangement by working from the outside, in, center and back out. All the while making it loosely rounded. The astilbe will be in the center. This sounds more complicated than it is—trust me!

**5** The astilbe with it's plume should be the tallest flower and in the center of the bouquet. Turn your wrist and check the arrangement from all sides.

**6** Fluff and rearrange the flowers and berries as you see fit.

**7** Once you have the flowers arranged as you like them, hold your thumb on the front of the bouquet stems.

**8** Slide the end of a 20-inch piece of twine under your thumb, leaving about 6 inches dangling.

**9** Tighten your grip a bit as you wrap the twine around the bunch of stems two or three times.

**10** Lay the wrapped stems on the table gently tie the twine into a bow. Clip off the extra twine ends. *Don't use your floral shears!*

**11** Now take your floral shears and trim the stem ends to the same length and on a 45-degree angle.

**12** Slip the tied bouquet into the Mason jar so the bow is submerged. *A little twist on your usual twine tied jar!*

## SEPTEMBER TIPS

Astilbe has very thin and fragile stems, so be careful not to bend or damage the stems as that may prevent water from traveling to the flower head.

Don't get frustrated when building the bouquet in your palm. It may take a few tries and practice to get it down. *I know you can do it!*

Make a few, send them to school with your kids for teachers, or place at a friend's door for a lovely surprise. Ring and run, but turn back to see the smile of their faces when they see the bouquet!

*"It is only goodness which gives extras, and so I say again, that we have much to hope for from flowers. "*

Sir Arthur Conan Doyle

# OCTOBER

Please know I adore pumpkins. In a patch, on my porch in my floral designs, but for our October arrangement I decided to go sans pumpkin in favor of a little 'hay bale'. Come October you can create this design and pile up pumpkins all around the base. That would be so darling!

## October Flowers and Supplies

- One dozen small sunflowers

- Deep burgundy, almost chocolate colored ranunculus

- Four full sprigs of boxwood

- A large bag of green moss

- Three jars

- One rectangular wire basket 6–7 inches tall

# OCTOBER TUTORIAL

**1**   Line the wire basket with moss.

**2**   Slide the jars inside the moss-lined basket.

**3**   Fill the jars with treated water.

**4**   Place four sunflowers in each jar.

**5**   The sunflowers should be cut so they peek out of the moss, some almost appearing to rest on it.

**6**   Add 4–5 ranunculus per jar. Let the buds and flowers rise above the sunflowers at varying heights.

**7**   Tuck in two sprigs of boxwood at either end.

# October Tips

Choose sunflowers with black or dark brown centers.

Green moss looks best with this color combination, but with more orangey sunflowers and burnt orange ranunculus, the fawn colored Spanish moss would be a lovely choice.

To freshen the water: remove each jar, lift out the flowers, and pour the original water out. Refill with treated water and fluff the moss.

If you'd like, tuck in some baby boo pumpkins pierced with a chopstick or gather pumpkins at the base of the "hay bale". If you choose to add tiny pumpkins to the arrangement let them "sit" on the moss on both sides. Three on one side and two on the other would look best.

*"Every flower is a soul blossoming in nature."*

Gerard De Nerval

# November

November's arrangement happened by accident. I had another plan in mind for this month of thanks. Then I found myself giving "thanks" and plans changed.

I arrived later than usual at the flower mart. As I was paying for my bouquets, the cashier motioned to a wide cart laden with flowers and said, "If you want any of those, just take 'em." My eyes went wide and I replied, "Just take them?" His response: "Yup, they are headed to the trash. They are from yesterday. We are closing and can't sell them tomorrow."

On hearing those words, I am pretty sure I started to sweat. I know my head swirled with all the possibilities as I gazed upon that giant cart, including how could I attach it to the bumper of my car!

With many words of thanks, I headed over to pick out what I wanted. There were many kinds of flowers. They all looked pretty good to me, and I knew I could revive any droopy ones with a good conditioning at home. I didn't want to leave any behind, but with my cart full already, I had to make choices. I was drawn to the fading hydrangeas and decided to take orchids that I normally would not buy. I managed to grab a few bunches of wax flower too.

Then someone on the other side started moving the cart. My browsing was over. I turned to thank the cashier again. He was already gone—when your day starts at 2 a.m., 10 a.m. is quitting time.

Well, *my* day was just really getting going, now that I had a whole new plan for November. I headed home and this is the design I came up with for us...it is truly full of thanks.

# November Flowers and Supplies

- 6–8 fading hydrangea (perfect if you pick them in September/October from your garden and let them dry, or simply let them fade in the garden.)

- 4 long stems of maroon cymbidium orchids

- 1/4 bunch wax flower or other wispy filler flower

- 1/2 bunch snowball feverfew or other small creamy white flower

- A few stems of coffee bean berries in white and green.

- 4 medium length branches in dark brown

- A rectangular box, about 20 inches long with liner

- Floral foam

- Florists tape

# November Tutorial

**1** If your planter/box is not lined, insert some plastic food storage containers to hold the water.

**2** Wedge in foam, and, if not secure, fasten down with florist's tape.

**3** Add treated cool water. Orchids prefer cool water and the other flowers in this arrangement won't mind.

**4** Insert 3 or 4 hydrangeas on each side for a total of 6–8 hydrangeas. The planter/box should appear full already.

**5** The orchid stems will drape across the front of both sides of the planter. To make this happen, insert the left-draping stems on the far right, about two to three inches from the right end. Then insert the right-draping stems on the far left about two to three inches from the left end. The orchid stems will cross each other, filling the bottom of the design with flowers and drape elegantly off each side.

**6** Tuck in wax flower, snowball feverfew, and green berries in the center on each side. Cluster bunches for greater impact.

**7** On an angle, insert two branches and two white berry stems at varying heights on each end. The branches and white berries should be flaring out and up.

**8** Place the arrangement on your table and give thanks!

187

# NOVEMBER TIPS

To dry hydrangeas you can harvest and hang them upside down in a cool dark place or just do what I do, simply place them in individual vases without any water. Oh my, that sounds cruel, but it works. They don't get misshapen as they are not squished together and you get to enjoy them while they dry out.

In order to get the faded autumn colored hydrangeas I used here, leave them on the bushes until the color naturally fades. Pick and dry when the coloring is right for you.

Cymbidium orchids are look exotic, but don't equate exotic with high maintenance. These flowers are strong and have a long vase life. Cymbidiums can last 15-20 days in a vase. Remember, as I mentioned, they prefer cool water.

*"Don't spend your life waiting for someone to send you flowers, make your own arrangements."*

Kelly Wilkniss

# DECEMBER

The combination of silver and red roses is so elegant and befitting of the holidays. For this rich combination, the roses should be a deep velvety red and the silver aged with patina. Combine the roses & silver with crisp white and berries you have the perfect December arrangement.

Designed in three containers, our December design will suit all your holiday entertaining needs. Display it all together, or break it apart and move it around the house wherever you need a beautiful festive pop.

Eggnog on the porch? Bring the small container out on a tray. Cocktails in the living room? Place the medium-sized vase on the coffee table. Leave the large one on a table in the entry. Then bring them all back together on the dining room table for a buffet. For a sit-down dinner, the tall arrangement alone would be lovely flanked with a trio of different sized candles. If it is narrow enough and 24 inches or more in height, it won't obstruct the view across the table very much. The medium and small ones can then be positioned on a sideboard or in the kitchen—as you know, people will end up in there no matter what you do!

# December Flowers and Supplies

- One dozen red roses

- Ten stems of freesia

- A bunch of myrtle

- Red coffee bean berries a.k.a. hypericum

- Three silver/silver-plated pitchers of different sizes

# December Tutorial

1  Fill the silver pitchers/containers with treated water.

2  Strip the bottom leaves off the myrtle stems. Any leaves below the water line must go. Trim the myrtle so it stands about double the height or more of the vase you are filling.

3  With the deep green myrtle stems, create the foundation of your arrangement. You can use any long-stemmed deep green foliage.

4  Add freesia to the medium and tall containers, making sure the arching unopened buds are extending outward.

5  Now come the roses: place five roses in each of the bigger containers, and two in the small container.

6  Tuck in the berry stems to all three, making sure they are spread throughout each container.

## December Tips

Pick up silver-plated urns, pitchers, and sugar bowls for a few dollars at thrift stores and yard sales. You can even spray-paint vases that you already have metallic silver or gold for a similar look.

When adding the freesia, for best effect, position one so it drapes over the small vase when all three are clustered together.

As you may be separating these containers to use on their own, move them apart to make sure they each are arranged to stand alone as well as together.

# Conclusion

What a delight it has been to write this book, design the arrangements for the tutorials and spend time with you in mind. My hope is that you have enjoyed reading these pages as much as I enjoyed the process of creating them.

Moreover, my hope is that by reading this book you have gained the knowledge, confidence & skill to make not only these 12 arrangements, but countless beautiful florals in the many years to come. Florals that will elevate your everyday, make someone else smile and maybe even grace special events. I know you can do all that and more with your talent, imagination and the practical information you learned here. So go on start designing! When you do send me a photo or two I would truly love to see the arrangements you create. I will look out for all that beauty at kellymysoulfulhome@gmail.com

Here's to creating beauty!

xo,

Kelly

# THANK YOU/ACKNOWLEDGEMENTS

Thank you to my family who cheered me on and patiently waited for "after the book is written..." for many things. *Sometimes even dinner ;)*

Thank you to my mom & the few friends I shared my secret with for making me believe I could write a whole book.

Thank you to Anita & Yvonne for totally getting 'it' and giving wonderful advice.

Thank you to Trish Reda for the photos of me. Your talent, humor and encouragement helped enormously. It would have been really hard to take photos of myself while arranging flowers ~ and no way would I have been laughing while doing it!

...and last, but certainly not least, for without him this book would not exist, thank you to Glynn and Passageway Press for finding my blog, reading my writing and offering to make a dream reality. *I am still pinching myself Glynn!*

# CHECKLIST FOR LONG LASTING CUT FLOWERS

☐    Buy the freshest flowers you can get your hands on.

☐    Prepare a container of treated lukewarm water. Use cool water for orchids, chrysanthemums, bouvardia, and bulb flowers.

☐    Let flowers sit in a cool, dark place to rehydrate for a minimum of two hours.

☐    Fill the display vase/container with treated water.

☐    If necessary, make second cut for the arrangement in the same manner as first cut. Do not recut daffodils.

☐    Design: have fun!

☐    Stand back and admire!

☐    Change the water and add fresh preservative every three days.

## Author Biography

Kelly lives in Pasadena California with her husband, two girls, and Emmett, their faithful & feisty Maltese. She is lovingly restoring an 1886 Victorian farmhouse, which you can see on her blog. If everyone had a motto Kelly's would be: Be kind, work hard and see the beauty.

If you enjoyed this book you can find more by Kelly at her blog, app or podcast.

mysoulfulhome.com (the blog)
bHome.us (the app)
decoratingtipsandtricks.com (the podcast)

*I've included some blank pages for you to make notes on your own floral experiences and adventures.*

*Good luck!*

*xo*

*Kelly*

CPSIA information can be obtained
at www.ICGtesting.com
Printed in the USA
BVOW05*1201070817
491283BV00013B/63/P

9 781334 999086